Professional Development

Sitton Spelling and Word Skills®
Seminar Handbook
Grades 1–8

2009–2010 edition

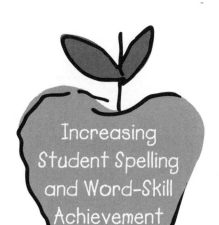

Increasing Student Spelling and Word-Skill Achievement

EDUCATORS PUBLISHING SERVICE
Cambridge and Toronto

FOR YOUR INFORMATION

THIS IS THE SEMINAR HANDBOOK.

Sitton Spelling and Word Skills® Seminar Handbook
Increasing Student Spelling and Word-Skill Achievement
2009-2010 Edition

Illustrator: Donna Bernard

888-WE-SPELL
www.epsbooks.com/sittonspelling

Printed in USA

ISBN 978-1-886050-78-5

2 3 4 5 PPG 12 11 10 09

Table of Contents

Welcome!

Today the water is going to be tested. We'll inspect the results. We won't stop there. We'll develop a plan to install a new water system. One that works. One that meets our standards for water purity. One backed up by evidence that proves it filters the particles that produce the problems. Alas! Why did we tolerate this for so long?

Why do students spell well on a word-list test but cannot spell the same words correctly in everyday writing? Why aren't we getting the results we want?

Today's seminar focuses on a solution to this dilemma that frustrates teachers most about spelling. Before our seminar starts, speculate on an answer—write your answer. Then listen up today. At the end of the day, let's see whether new insights have helped you discover a solution.

My answer to the question *before* the seminar—

Because…

My answer to the question *after* the seminar—

Because…

1

Can we make a difference?

If we want students to learn to spell with accuracy in their everyday writing, we can do it. But we cannot pretend to be interested in helping students toward this end if we continue to use strategies and procedures that our own experience tells us do not work.

The single biggest influence on student achievement is this—*teachers*! Teachers—what they teach, and how they teach it—*make the difference*. So, *yes*, teachers can *make a significant difference* using best practices instruction for teaching spelling and word skills!

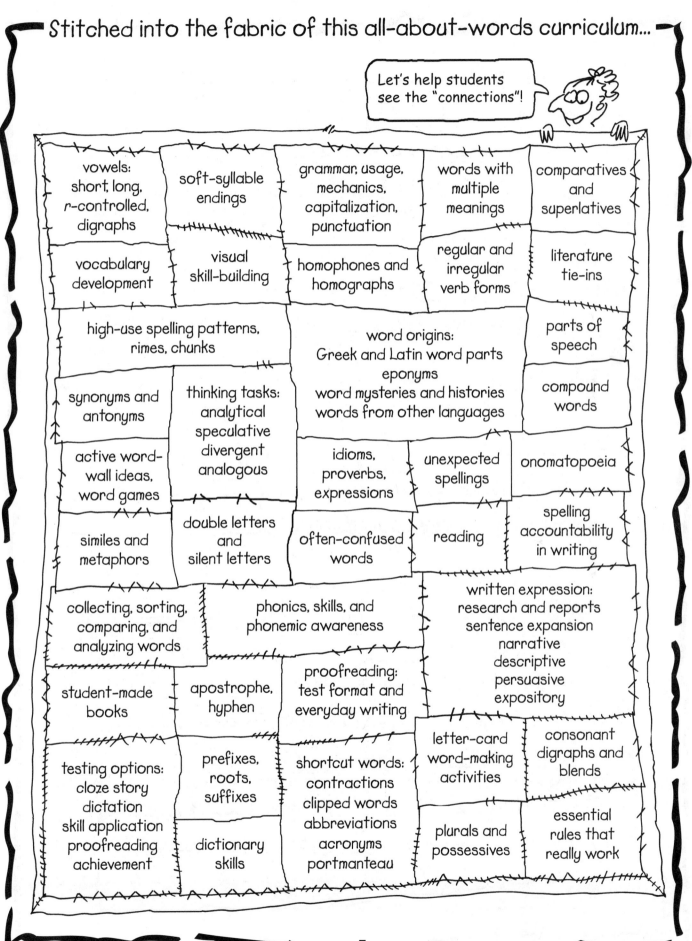

Let's help students see the "connections"!

vowels: short, long, r-controlled, digraphs

soft-syllable endings

grammar, usage, mechanics, capitalization, punctuation

words with multiple meanings

comparatives and superlatives

vocabulary development

visual skill-building

homophones and homographs

regular and irregular verb forms

literature tie-ins

high-use spelling patterns, rimes, chunks

word origins: Greek and Latin word parts eponyms word mysteries and histories words from other languages

parts of speech

synonyms and antonyms

thinking tasks: analytical speculative divergent analogous

compound words

active word-wall ideas, word games

idioms, proverbs, expressions

unexpected spellings

onomatopoeia

similes and metaphors

double letters and silent letters

often-confused words

reading

spelling accountability in writing

collecting, sorting, comparing, and analyzing words

phonics, skills, and phonemic awareness

written expression: research and reports sentence expansion narrative descriptive persuasive expository

student-made books

apostrophe, hyphen

proofreading: test format and everyday writing

testing options: cloze story dictation skill application proofreading achievement

prefixes, roots, suffixes

shortcut words: contractions clipped words abbreviations acronyms portmanteau

letter-card word-making activities

consonant digraphs and blends

dictionary skills

plurals and possessives

essential rules that really work

We must teach students ___how___ to spell and proofread.

Then be concise about ___What___ to do.

One set of how-to skills are the ___Visual skills___.

The two procedures that research says are the best ways to develop these skills are:

1. ___Independt Word   Study___
   5 steps: Read, spell, Cover, Print, Check (p. 86)

2. ___Pretest___

The ___Pretest___ is not a ___test___.

It is a ___Practice activity___.

We will call it the ___Word Preview___.

Before our demonstration, do this activity that points out the purpose of the demonstration—

Three Things to Remember

First, the procedure develops ___Visual skills___.

Second, the procedure provides an opportunity to teach and practice

a ___Strategy___ for learning and proofreading ___any word___.

Third, the procedure is not a ___test___!

Build Visual Skills

Do the Word Preview, a visual warm-up activity, with all students. (See pages 154-155 for blackline masters.)

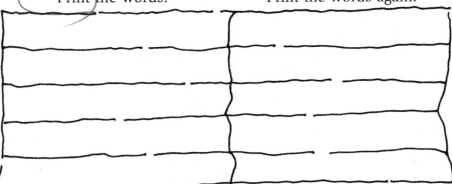

Print the words.   Print the words again.

The research-based steps for administering the Word Preview need to be followed carefully to get the best results in the least amount of time.

Teacher	Students
1. Says the word. Says the word in a sentence. Says the word again.	1. Look at, and listen to, the teacher. *Pencils down*
2. Asks students to write the word.	2. Print the word in the write (left-hand) column of their paper.

After students have written the words, guide them as they check their own paper.

Teacher	Students
3. Spells the word aloud.	3. Proofread the word by touching each letter with the point of their pencil as the letter name is said. Circle errors.
4. Prints the word on the board, saying the name of each letter as it is printed. *pencils down!*	4. Look at the chalkboard and listen to the teacher.
5. Observes students.	5. Rewrite the word in the rewrite (right-hand) column of their paper.

By the way—
- it's best to give all the words—then correct.
- we'll identify specific words for the Word Preview later.
- a time line will be provided for how often to administer the Word Preview.
- all students take the Word Preview.
- words on the Word Preview are NOT the Spelling Words.

Why do we develop visual skills in the Word Preview?

 Research says that good spellers have the ability to see the sequential letters of words in their mind's eye.

> This can be taught and learned.

 Research says that good spellers have the ability to focus attention on each sequential letter of a word.

> This can be taught and learned.

Research says that essential skills and strategies should be modeled and practiced before they can be successfully applied. These two strategies are taught and practiced during the Word Preview. Watch for how students will apply these skills with expectations for spelling and proofreading in their everyday writing—coming up later in your seminar.

Points to remember for the Word Preview.

- State concise expectations to students for taking the Word Preview.
- The Word Preview should be fast-paced and brief. Use three words for Grade 1 and five words for Grade 2 and above.
- Students should *print*, to accentuate each letter as a separate unit.
- Students should print the word in the "rewrite" column (right-hand column) without the benefit of hearing the letters said aloud as they write.
- Check only the "rewrite" column.
- After the Word Preview has been checked, the paper need not be saved. It is the process, not the product, that is important.
- Remember—the Word Preview words are **not the Spelling Words**. They should not be posted following the Word Preview, and they should not be sent home. The purpose of the Word Preview is to teach and practice visual skills, not to introduce or pretest Spelling Words.

FOR YOUR INFORMATION

Check it out later—

- how to administer the Word Preview   pages 44–45
- more visual skill building   pages 46–47
- students challenged with the Word Preview   pages 77–79

headline states the objective

Build Skills and Word Experiences

UNIT 17

Use Student Practice Pages 49–50 to follow up instruction for:
Activity 1A • Activities 3A, 3B

pencil signals activities that have correlated student Practice Book pages—*optional* (see page 161)

Build Visual Skills

WORD PREVIEW

Do the Word Preview, a visual warm-up activity, with all students.
Use Core Words **sure** (251), **knew** (252), **it's** (253), **try** (254), **told** (255).

Teaching Notes, page 331

five-minute visual-skill warm-up—**_not_** *optional* (see pages 44–45)

Build Spelling and Language Skills

EXERCISE EXPRESS

Choose from among these quick tasks to customize instruction for all or selected students.

Teaching Notes, page 334

"sponge" activities to use anytime throughout the unit, or later in subsequent units— *optional* (see pages 48–49)

STRETCH IT — It's across the way.

FIX IT — What was that sound. Father tolld the children to try there best to keep very still. Soon they all new for shure that it was only the water.
(question mark, *told*, *their*, *knew*, *sure*)

SORT IT — knew, right, sure, come, light, know, large, high, have
(e.g., silent letter *k*/*gh*/*e*; number of letters)

ADD IT — my, try, by, why, _____, _____, _____, _____
(words that end in long *i* spelled *y*)

FINISH IT — It's always hard for me to tell my mother _____.

FIND IT — Words that show possession, or ownership
(e.g., Mary's, theirs, its)

161

REPLACE IT — Replace It, in Levels 7–8, is a synonym activity for "worn out" words— *optional* (see page 49)

 Which words are used on the Word Preview?

👁 the same words used for teaching all essential skills and concepts

👁 high-frequency writing words

These words have a name: _____

These words have two purposes:

1. _teach skills and concepts_

2. (This purpose comes later. Not to worry, now.)

2.

core words are not the program

HIGH-FREQUENCY CORE WORDS

FOR TEACHING SKILLS AND CONCEPTS

Grade Level 1   High-Frequency Core Words 1–35

→ Grade Level 2   High-Frequency Core Words 36–170

Grade Level 3   High-Frequency Core Words 171–335

Grade Level 4   High-Frequency Core Words 336–500

Grade Level 5   High-Frequency Core Words 501–675

Grade Level 6   High-Frequency Core Words 676–850

Grade Level 7   High-Frequency Core Words 851–1025

Grade Level 8   High-Frequency Core Words 1026–1200

no overlap

FOR YOUR INFORMATION

The high-frequency Core Words for teaching skills and concepts

at my grade level are _____ .

3.

High-frequency Core Words are *not* the _spelling words_.

👁 These are words used in the Build Skills and Word Experiences part of a unit to grow all the essential skills and concepts. As we grow these skills and concepts, we are *not* teaching specific words.

 "core words" are seeds, not the program

4 Why do we need to grow skills and concepts?

- 👁 A reading program is not <u>List g words</u>.

- 👁 A spelling program is not <u>List g words</u>.

- 👁 If you think of spelling as "teaching words," you'll be disappointed with the results.

It's Monday! HERE ARE YOUR WORDS.

For now, teach "general word skills." These are the strategies to help students gain insights into how all words work. A focus on "specific words" comes later.

5 Which skills and concepts do we teach?

- 👁 Teachers, as *practitioners*, select skills and concepts. They craft a spelling curriculum *their* way—one aligned with their state standards, integrated with their existing communications curriculum materials, and *differentiated* to meet the needs of all ability levels.

6 How does a "word" approach differ from a "skills and concepts" approach?

Here comes the demonstration! WATCH AND LISTEN.

Kids will: collect, analyze, generalize (rule or concept) and expand. (exceptions)

EXAMPLES of CONCEPTS and ACTIVITIES that SUPPORT THEM

1. Some words are spelled the way they sound, while others are not.

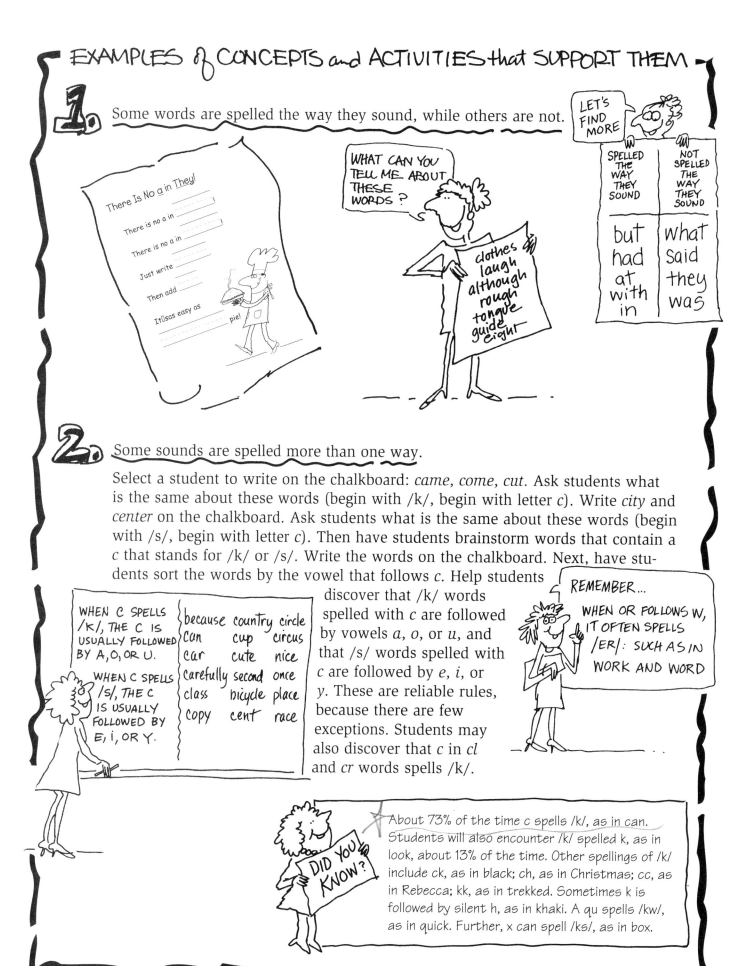

There Is No *a* in *They*!

There is no a in _____
There is no a in _____
Just write _____
Then add _____
It's as easy as _____ pie!

WHAT CAN YOU TELL ME ABOUT THESE WORDS?

clothes
laugh
although
rough
tongue
guide
eight

LET'S FIND MORE

SPELLED THE WAY THEY SOUND	NOT SPELLED THE WAY THEY SOUND
but had at with in	what said they was

2. Some sounds are spelled more than one way.

Select a student to write on the chalkboard: *came, come, cut*. Ask students what is the same about these words (begin with /k/, begin with letter *c*). Write *city* and *center* on the chalkboard. Ask students what is the same about these words (begin with /s/, begin with letter *c*). Then have students brainstorm words that contain a *c* that stands for /k/ or /s/. Write the words on the chalkboard. Next, have students sort the words by the vowel that follows *c*. Help students discover that /k/ words spelled with *c* are followed by vowels *a*, *o*, or *u*, and that /s/ words spelled with *c* are followed by *e*, *i*, or *y*. These are reliable rules, because there are few exceptions. Students may also discover that *c* in *cl* and *cr* words spells /k/.

WHEN C SPELLS /K/, THE C IS USUALLY FOLLOWED BY A, O, OR U.

WHEN C SPELLS /S/, THE C IS USUALLY FOLLOWED BY E, I, OR Y.

because	country	circle
can	cup	circus
car	cute	nice
carefully	second	once
class	bicycle	place
copy	cent	race

REMEMBER... WHEN OR FOLLOWS W, IT OFTEN SPELLS /ER/: SUCH AS IN WORK AND WORD

DID YOU KNOW? About 73% of the time c spells /k/, as in can. Students will also encounter /k/ spelled k, as in look, about 13% of the time. Other spellings of /k/ include ck, as in black; ch, as in Christmas; cc, as in Rebecca; kk, as in trekked. Sometimes k is followed by silent h, as in khaki. A qu spells /kw/, as in quick. Further, x can spell /ks/, as in box.

3. New words can be made by adding a prefix to the beginning of words and a suffix to the end of words.

 Give students ongoing experiences adding and subtracting prefixes and suffixes to/from base words. At every level, the rules that govern these changes need practice and expansion to incorporate a more sophisticated vocabulary. Generally, these rules are so consistent that students' spelling, as well as their vocabularies, can develop significantly with their use.

Help students understand that good spellers use this strategy: *Think about how to spell the base word* **first** *and then how to add the prefix and/or suffix.*

Make More Words

Add an ending
Tack it on!
Now take it off.
You see, it's gone!

Follow the rules,
You can't go wrong.
Make words short,
Or make them long.

no ending	s	ed	ing
help	helps	helped	helping
cook			
	shops		
		planned	
like			
			drying

LOOK FOR WORDS THAT END IN CONSONANT-Y BECAUSE THERE'S A VERY GOOD REASON WHY!

APPLY IDENTITY COMPANY

took!

 Teach students to identify and spell the few exceptions to the basic suffix rules.

DID YOU KNOW?

A prefix changes the meaning of words. When a prefix is added to the beginning of a word, the spelling of the base word never changes—make/remake. A suffix changes the part of speech of words. Sometimes when a suffix is added to the end of a word, the spelling of the base word changes—make/making.

4. Some words have silent letters,

...but, sometimes silent letters have a purpose.

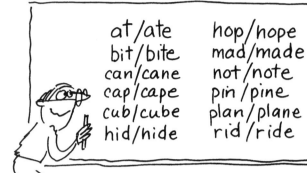

at / ate	hop / nope
bit / bite	mad / made
can / cane	not / note
cap / cape	pin / pine
cub / cube	plan / plane
hid / hide	rid / ride

AN APOSTROPHE HAS A PURPOSE...

 5. An apostrophe is used in a contraction and in some possessives.

- TO TAKE THE PLACE OF A LETTER OR LETTERS IN A CONTRACTION.
- TO SHOW OWNERSHIP.

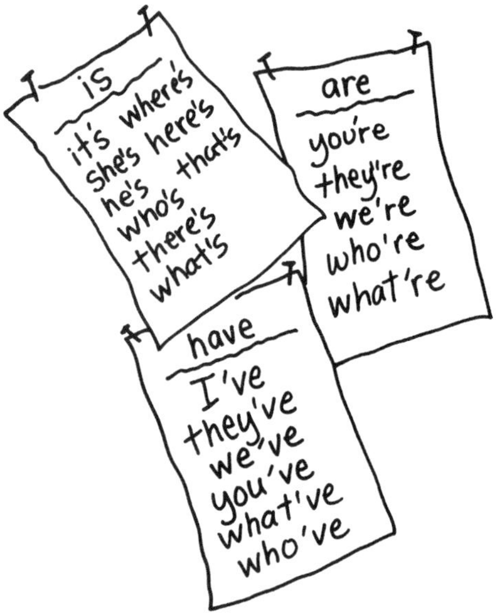

is
it's   where's
she's   here's
he's   who's   that's
there's
what's

are
you're
they're
we're
who're
what're

have
I've
they've
we've
you've
what've
who've

SO, HOW MANY BROTHERS AND HOW MANY FRIENDS?

I gave my friend's books to my brothers' teachers.
I gave my friends' books to my brother's teachers.
I gave my friend's books to my brother's teachers.
I gave my friends' books to my brothers' teachers.

6 Double letters spell one sound.

A concept begins _____, then grows to more sophisticated discoveries.

Stellaluna
Little Red Riding Hood
Tikki Tikki Tembo
Anno
Cinderella

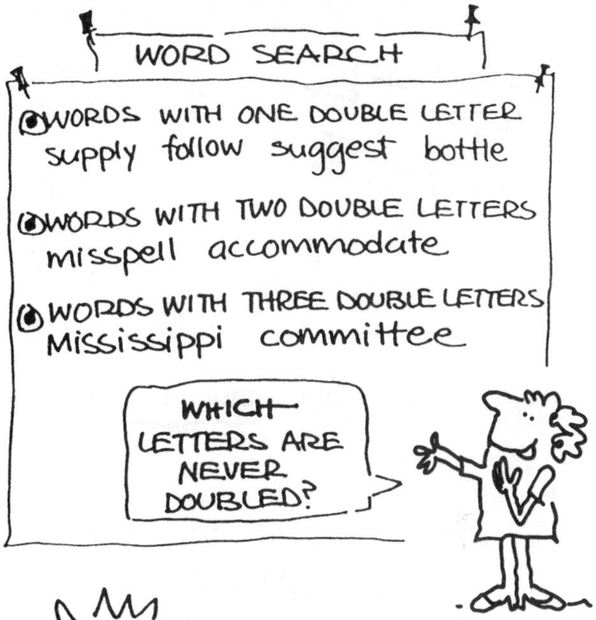

WORD SEARCH

● WORDS WITH ONE DOUBLE LETTER
supply follow suggest bottle

● WORDS WITH TWO DOUBLE LETTERS
misspell accommodate

● WORDS WITH THREE DOUBLE LETTERS
Mississippi committee

WHICH LETTERS ARE NEVER DOUBLED?

7 Some words have more than one meaning.

BAT

SOME WORDS HAVE MORE THAN ONE MEANING...

BEGINNING —
stray
street
straight

streak
strong
structure

MIDDLE —
Australia
apostrophe
construct

ENDING —

8 Some words are spelled with consonant blends.

NOW FOR WORDS THAT END WITH STR!

Homophones are words that sound the same but have different meanings and spellings.

TO MASTER HOMOPHONES,

THE FIRST STEP IS TO LEARN TO IDENTIFY THEM...

THEN LEARN TO DIFFERENTIATE THEIR MEANINGS...

THEN LEARN TO SPELL THEM.

...and then there are homophone contractions!

IF IT MAKES SENSE TO SAY "THERE IS," USE THERE'S...IF NOT, USE THEIRS.

IF IT MAKES SENSE TO SAY "IT IS," USE IT'S...IF NOT, USE ITS!

...and then there are homographs—make a homograph accordion book on sturdy paper. Students write sentences and illustrate the meanings—wind, tear, close, project, lead, object, desert, does, contest, bow, conduct, record, perfect, use, content, read, minute...

A knowledge of Greek and Latin roots unlocks the meaning of many words.

LATIN ROOTS WE KNOW—

voc — call
vocabulary

port — carry
transport

ped — foot
pedestrian

struct — build
construct

 A strategic speller uses a knowledge of the most frequent spelling patterns.

Spelling Long a

a	ai	ay	a-consonant-e	other
baby	afraid	maybe	came	eight
paper	plain	day	page	they
	grain	play	parade	
	main	gray	blaze	

Spelling Long e

e	ee	ea	y	other
me	see	each	Billy	people
we	feet	eat	easy	these
before	keep	read	baby	Susie
she	three	east	many	
he	need	team		

Spelling Long i

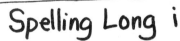

i	y	igh	ind	i-consonant-e	other
tiger	my	high	find	time	pie
lion	try	right	kind	dime	
	cry	light	grind	like	
	why	night	mind	bite	
	fly	fight	wind	line	

12. A compound word is a combination of two or more words.

 high + way = highway

b Make a bulletin board of compound word equations.

pop + corn = popcorn

star + fish = starfish

 said

whispered

13. Synonyms are words that have similar meanings.

yelled whined shouted

HOW BIG?

big huge
large great
gigantic
enormous
immense
jumbo

14. Antonyms are words with opposite meanings.

 ANTONYMS ARE OPPOSITE WORDS

lengthen shorten

15. Analogous thinking aids spelling.

 analogous spelling

DID YOU KNOW?

The study of high-frequency spelling patterns, or rimes, is a sensible, research-based strategy to generate hundreds of words. Several respected educators (including Wylie and Durrell, Edward Fry, and Marilyn Adams) have identified 35–40 rimes that can form up to 650 different one-syllable primary words. These key rimes are taught and recycled continuously through the first two levels of the Sourcebook Series and then occur intermittently for reinforcement at subsequent levels.

__ay, __ill, __ip, __at, __am, __ag, __ack, __ank, __ick, __ell, __ot, __ing, __ap, __y, __unk, __ail, __ain, __eed, __ice, __out, __ug, __op, __in, __an, __est, __ink, __ow, __ew, __ore, __ed, __ab, __ob, __ock, __ake, __ine, __ight, __im, __uck, __um/p.

THE SKILLS AND CONCEPTS CAN BE CULTIVATED THROUGH MULTIPLE STRATEGIES. CHECK OUT THESE EXAMPLES —

USE MANIPULATIVES

s t a y

th at

How wh ch en ere ip sh

one for won

h e r

Have students make words, make sentences. Word-making activities with letter and word card blackline masters are in the SOURCEBOOKS.

USE ACTIVE VISUALS 2

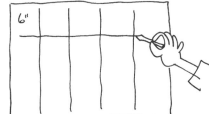

SURPRISE WORDS

Read |said| See |said|

It's a spelling surprise!
To spell |said| correctly,
I have to use my eyes!

|was| |they| |what|

Other word choices may include:

another—then, than, net, hot, hat, rat, ton, rot, ran, tan, heat, neat, tea, ten, hen

something—set, site, get, gets, might, sight, night, time, stem, sting, home, those, most, ten, this, him, mist

threesome—more, term, sort, theme, most, mesh, moth, meet, the, so, set, met, he, sheet, shot, rest

without—with, it, thou, out, tow, tout, oh, tot

workshop—pow, sow, sop, whoop, show, so, pork, oh, how, row, hops, hook, shook, who, rows, hoops

another	something	threesome	without	workshop
a	some	three	hit	work
an	me	threes	hut	works
not	met	some	hot	or
note	thin	me	to	shop
other	thing	see	who	hop
the	the	tree	two	hoop
he	then	trees	how	poor
her	them	seem	wit	posh

Use the Ten-Box Reusable Chart (directions below) for word collections. Above, students collect words they can make using the letters of compound words. The chart is created with large and small post-it notes.

1 Cut a piece of poster board or oil cloth.

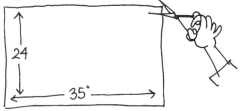

2 Measure and mark 7" increments across the width. Make vertical lines at each mark using colored tape or a marker. This will divide your chart into five equal columns.

3 Measuring 6" from the top, make a horizontal rule using colored tape or a marker. You now have a Ten-Box Reusable Chart. The top five boxes will each hold a large sticky note, and the lower five boxes have room for many small ones.

USE RHYMES

3

CONTEXT SENTENCES MAY HELP YOUR STUDENTS WITH ARE/OUR/HOUR...

Our frogs are sleeping by the lake. In one hour they'll be awake!

YES! YES! YES!

For words that end in consonant-*y*
That you would like to multiply,
Forget the math and just do this—
Change *y* to *i* and add *es*!

But if a vowel comes before the *y*,
Here's the rule that you'll apply.
Just write the word and then add *s*.
Can you do it? Yes! Yes! Yes!

In *why* and *fly*, *y* says long *i*.
In *yes* it stands for the consonant *y*.
But watch *y* change and say long *e*,
In many words, like *family*.

Beautiful Advice

I have some advice that I enjoy telling.
It will help you avoid a common misspelling—
When adding the suffix that means *full of*,
Write only one *l*; give the other a shove.
If something is full of beauty, my friend,
Then a beautiful spelling has one *l* at the end.

ALL THE ACTIVITY EXAMPLES HAVE COME FROM THE SOURCEBOOK SERIES

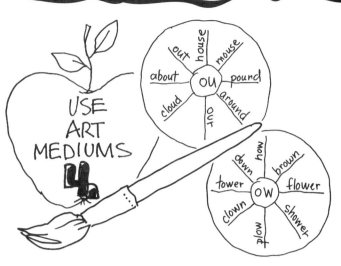

USE
ART
MEDIUMS
4.

 Have students explain and <u>illustrate</u> idioms, proverbs, famous quotations.

History repeats itself.
This means that —

USE
GAMES
5.

Write *place* and *nice* on the chalkboard. Underline *ce*. Point out that *c* spells /s/ when it is followed by *e*. Then write on the chalkboard _*ace* and _*ice*. Ask students which word pattern they think will win the race. Have students take turns writing words on the chalkboard to see which pattern produces a longer list.

 Name a three-syllable word of Spanish origin that can be worn.

MYSTERY
WORD

_ _ _ _ b _ _ _ _ _

22

Provide spelling strategies, such as clever rhymes and phrases—the princi**pal** is your **pal**, fri**end** to the **end**, **pie**ce of **pie**, **for**ty **for**ts.

USE MNEMONIC DEVICES
6a

HEAR WITH YOUR **EAR**.
HERE AND **THERE**
ARE PLACES.

One day I saw an elephant.
He stood on his hind legs
And looked at me and shouted,
"I want my scrambled eggs!"

This elephant had a secret,
I'm just about to tell.
Big elephants can always use
Scrambled eggs to learn to spell—
b-e-c-a-u-s-e—
Because!

USE LITERATURE and MAKE BOOKS
7a

Relate literature to learning to spell. Have students make books to apply spelling skills—perhaps CANNED BOOKS in which students write their stories on adding machine tape to coil inside a clean soup can. Then they decorate the can by making a colorful label with the book's title.

OUR ONLY MAY AMELIA
Jennifer Holm

USE
THINKING
SKILLS

Explain: What determines the ending letter—*k*, *ck*, or *ke*? Explain the concept.

State reasons: What do you think causes proofreading errors for words that the writer knows how to spell? State reasons with examples.

Make analogies:

Antonyms—*Before* is to *after* as *inside* is to o_____.
Synonyms—*Common* is to *ordinary* as *frightened* is to a_____.
Part to Whole—*Bulb* is to *lamp* as *limb* is to t_____.
Classification—*Truck* is to *vehicle* as *schooner* is to b_____.
Characteristic—*Sticky* is to *glue* as *sweet* is to s_____.
Function—*Shovel* is to *dig* as *credit card* is to ch_____.
Degree—*Hot* is to *boiling* as *map* is to an a_____.

Sequence: *foot, feet, person, people, goose,* _____, _____, _____.

HOW ARE THEY ALIKE? HOW ARE THEY DIFFERENT?

Compare and contrast: How are these alike? How are they different?

naming words	doing words
NOUNS	VERBS
church	munch
inch	touch
lunch	pinch
bench	punch
ranch	watch
branch	itch
witch	hatch
match	stitch
switch	scratch
	catch
	stretch

Draw conclusions: Based on what we know about nouns and verbs—

WHICH WORDS CAN BE A NOUN OR A VERB?

Speculate: What would happen if we had no homophones?

Evaluate: Do you think having a Spell Check reference is helpful? Why or why not?

Judge: From looking at this list of words, which rule best states the action taken to add the suffix?

Hypothesize: Which ending pattern, ___*ise* or ___*ize,* occurs most frequently?

● The seeds have been sown. Now for the harvest!

● What are the <u>benefits</u> of a skills and concepts approach?

Through the skills-and-concepts activities, students' insights about words evolve. They learn to construct spelling logic when they observe a word—not to just space out and see a sea of letters. When students begin to monitor their word experiences and to access the strategies they've been taught, they take a giant step forward toward becoming a strategic, independent, accurate speller.

Benefits of method

BASIC SKILLS and CONCEPTS	SPELLING LOGIC	MORE WORDS
STUDENTS' INVOLVEMENT	PARENT-CHILD PARTNER-SHIPS	FLEXIBILITY
BALANCED INSTRUCTION	INCREASED TEST SCORES	WRITING FLUENCY

p82–84

(For a review of the benefits, see page 51.)

Check it out later—
● For an overview of essentials skills and concepts by grade, see pages 52–59.
● For an overview of research-based concepts worth teaching, see pages 60–63.
● For a scope and sequence of essential skills by grade level, visit www.epsbooks.com/sittonspelling or see a grade-specific scope and sequence now included in each 3rd Edition Sourcebook.
● For more skills/concepts activities—INSTANT ACTIVITIES! They're waiting for you—for free—on blackline masters with teaching notes at www.sittonspelling.com.

What is and what is its purpose?

What determines which elements of language are included in Build Skillful Writers?

- Skills considered to be the most challenging for student writers.
- Skills most often tested on standardized achievement tests.

EXAMPLES OF TYPICAL TOPICS IN BUILD SKILLFUL WRITERS LEVELS 4–8

subject-verb agreement; comparatives/superlatives; metaphors/similes; abbreviations; compound sentences/conjunctions; idiomatic usage; letter/address formats; quotation marks/dialogue; persuasive writing techniques; double negatives; onomatopoeia; poetry terminology; writing narration, description, exposition; plural challenges; capitalization and punctuation; hyphenated words; dictionary pronunciation key; apostrophe use; portmanteau words; placement of modifiers; often-confused words (farther/further); using adjectives; contractions that are/aren't proper in writing; use of symbols in writing; using possessives; words with multiple meanings; repetition for emphasis/as redundancy; writing numbers; "uncluttering" your writing; placement of modifiers; words borrowed from other languages; using Latin expressions; homophone usage; transition words; using active verbs; tailoring writing to audience

What is  and what is its purpose?

Book Tie-Ins are included at every grade level.

What are  and —and what purpose do they serve?

Vocabulary development options are in every unit at every grade level.

Skills and concepts are revisited—

- within each level: layer upon layer, students develop understandings

- from level to level: all skills and concepts are reviewed, then expanded

<u>Research says—</u>

 Exposure of skills in small increments over time is clearly superior to a one-time major focus on a skill.

SKILLS NEED TO BE

- ## TAUGHT
- ## PRACTICED
- ## RECYCLED
- ## TESTED

Teachers—
Information you gather from your test results helps you to decide which skills and concepts to teach in subsequent units.

 What is  and what is its purpose?

 Test Ready is not optional. It "readies" students for the end-of-unit Skill Test.

 What is a Take-Home Task?

 There's a Take-Home Task in every unit at every level. Let's look.

 Then, we'll <u>walk through</u> Build Skills and Word Experiences in a unit.

The first part of every unit is <u>Build Skills and Word Experiences</u>—
"a focus on general word skills."

Now students have the foundation. Next, they apply their skills as they learn to spell specific words and to proofread for them in their writing!

English Grammar

SENTENCE SENSE

WORD USE
VOCABULARY

USE & ABUSE OF LANGUAGE

SOU BOOK

SPELLING
LITERATURE
PHONICS

<u>This part of a unit invests in all the communication skills.</u>

 The second part of every unit is <u>Assess Words and Skills</u>—
"a focus on specific word skills."

 Let's contrast customary assessment with assessment in this methodology.

Assessment in a customary program is _____ _____ _____ _____ .

<u>Features:</u>

1. _____

2. _____

3. _____

4. _____

5. _____

Is there an alternative assessment that maintains the positive, but eliminates the negative?
<u>Put your pencils down now.</u> Just listen. We'll fill in page 29 <u>together, later.</u>

The Spelling Words are the words _____ _____ _____.

They're studied at home on the _____ _____ ___ and at school in the

_____ _____ ___. All words are automatically recycled on subsequent
tests for automatic retesting to ensure mastery.

HIGH-FREQUENCY CORE WORDS FOR RECYCLING AND TESTING

Grade Level 1	1–35	Grade Level 5	1–675
Grade Level 2	1–170	Grade Level 6	1–850
Grade Level 3	1–335	Grade Level 7	1–1025
Grade Level 4	1–500	Grade Level 8	1–1200

FOR YOUR INFORMATION

The high-frequency Core Words recycled and tested at my

grade level are _1–170_____ .

Check it out later: More testing information, page 66.

LET'S FIND OUT MORE

 On page 10, we learned Core Words have two purposes. At that time, we
explored the first purpose. Now, we've noted the second purpose.
- First, Core Words grow the essential skills and concepts, as well as more
  words in Build Skills and Word Experiences.
- Second, Core Words grow_____ _____ ___.
  Core Words are the words that are tested in Assess Words and Skills.

 What constitutes a spelling unit, and is the unit organization the same at
all levels?

 What is the time frame for a spelling unit? See page 147. *you decide*
gr. 1   BSWE   5–6   AWS 2–3 days
gr. 2   "   "   "   "

 What happens if you don't "cover" every unit before the end of the year?

 Where do you begin when you start this program, and what "review" is
necessary before beginning? *Unit 1*
none

The Core Words are high-frequency writing words. How frequently are they used?

most misspelled words

Number of Words	Frequency of Use
8	18%
25	33%
100	50%
1200	90%

To increase the look of literacy in students' writing in the least time, with the least effort, select words for mastery in the order of frequency of use.

 In which bank of high-frequency writing words are most spelling errors made?

 What often overlooked factor is a certain contributor to students' spelling errors in writing?

Lack of expectations

 What should be expected of students for spelling accountability in their writing?

 writing process ___100%___

⬤ everyday writing

1. ___topical words___
2. ___high frequency___

 How can we teach students that spelling well in writing is necessary, and *expected*?

Priority words

What are <u>Priority Words</u>?
Let's find out!

PRIORITY WORDS

Priority Words are high-frequency Core Words that are designated as "no excuses" words and cannot be missed in writing—ever!

PRIORITY WORDS
FOR 100% ACCOUNTABILITY BY <u>END OF YEAR</u>

Grade Level 1   High-Frequency Core Words 1–15*
→ Grade Level 2   High-Frequency Core Words 1–35
Grade Level 3   High-Frequency Core Words 1–55**
Grade Level 4   High-Frequency Core Words 1–75***
Grade Level 5   High-Frequency Core Words 1–100****
Grade Levels 6–8   High-Frequency Core Words 1–130

     * include to/two, but omit too until Grade 2
    ** omit there/their/they're and your/you're until Grade 4
   *** add there/their/they're and your/you're
**** add there's/theirs

FOR YOUR INFORMATION

The Priority Words at my grade level by the <u>END</u> of the school year are _____1–35_____.

- ◗ an alphabetized reference *need this*

- ◗ minimum competency

- ◗ most students in a class have the same Priority Words *list, 2 lists 3 at the most*

- ◗ expectations require inspections

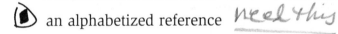

NO EXCUSES

> **It isn't** a list of the only words a student would be spelling correctly. **It is** a list of words that encompasses the words most frequently missed in writing.
>
> It is a **minimum proficiency** for spelling in everyday writing.
>
> As students proofread for these words, they practice the skills for **proofreading any word**—and they practice the skills necessary for scoring well on any **spelling achievement test.**

HOW MANY WORDS INITIATE A PRIORITY WORD LIST?

- too easy?   • First observe
- 100% standard
- how to introduce Priority Words
- time for proofreading

HOW DO YOU MARK A PAPER FOR PRIORITY WORDS?

- brackets
- other errors

WHAT ELSE DO I NEED TO KNOW ABOUT PRIORITY WORDS?

- folders
- parent-child partnerships
- figures into a grade
- an I-can-do-it approach

FOR YOUR INFORMATION

Check it out later—

- Organizing for Priority Words, see pages 69–72.

Formative Assessment—a good thing! Grading—often a necessary thing.

> Develop an assessment model with your grade-level team. The progress a student makes toward mastery is reflected in formative assessments, and this is often translated into a *grade*. But remember, grading is secondary (albeit often necessary) to the information formative tests gather and the action taken to target instruction to the tests' results that reflect students' needs.

Formative Assessments in this approach to spelling and word-skill literacy—

1. _Spelling in writing_

   Why? Because the goal of all spelling instruction is to help students spell in their everyday writing, so ongoing feedback regarding progress toward this goal is useful.

2. _unit tests a sentence dictation test_

   Why? Because targeting students' study to specific words they have not yet learned results in students' achievement toward their mastery.

3. _application skills_

   Why? Because information regarding students' acquisition of essential skills helps teachers select which skills to teach—what is taught has a high correlation to what is learned.

4. _Sourcebook activities_

   Why? Because student work that reflects their understanding of a concept provides concrete data about what they can do and can't do—nice to know before the next lesson is selected.

5. _practice book_

   Why? Here essential understandings are the focus, and as students complete the work a teacher learns how well each student is progressing toward competence.

6. _____

   Why? Because summative testing may negatively label a student unfairly if the testing situation is unfamiliar—and this formative test provides feedback toward students' test-wise progress.

👉 Which assessment(s) identifies students' differentiated list of Spelling Words?_____

👉 Which helps a teacher know how well students are applying higher-level thinking skills to the analysis and study of their Spelling Words? _____

👉 Which provides a teacher with ongoing information about how well students apply the skills they learned in the Word Preview?_____

(handwritten note in left margin: most important)

FOR YOUR LEISURE READING...

There is only so much anyone can tell you about how to ride a bicycle, play a card game, or use the Internet...

> And, there is only so much anyone can tell you about using the Sitton approach to spelling and word-skill literacy. To learn, you have to give it a try! There is no substitute for experience! Go for it!

Ideas for Getting Started

 Take action!
- Form a professional learning team, perhaps by grade. Review the seminar strategies together—collective effort is more powerful than working in isolation. The seminar jump-started your expertise—now, *use what you know so far*. Competence grows with experience.

 Tell students about the change.
- Explain how the routine will be different, and why.

 Inform parents of the change, and share with them how they can participate.
- See pages 82–85 (Seminar Handbook).
- Send home a copy of the Introducing Spelling Blackline Master (Sourcebook).
- Invite parents to view Introduction to Parents (Tutor Me Training® CD-ROM).
- Provide copies of the Core Words Blackline Master (Sourcebook).

 Make classroom preparations.
- Read One Teacher's Approach (Seminar Handbook, pages 112–118).
- Run blackline masters you choose to use regularly.
- Make Spelling Notebooks with students. (Spelling Notebooks are included in the Practice Books.)
- Review your "grade-level word banks" in this handbook, pages 10, 29, and 31.
- Use your grade-level Tutor Me CD-ROM for a complete walkthrough of Unit 1 (see page 166).

 Begin!
- Start on Unit 1, regardless of the time of year. No review is necessary. No need to rush!

 Talk it over.
- Routinely reconvene your learning team. Talk about what works, what doesn't. Once a consistent program has been implemented, all evidence on achievement points to you—*teachers*! And what does the research say about how teachers develop their internal expertise to improve instruction? It's *teachers in teams talking*—with a focused effort on a specific topic.
- If your professional learning team has questions, send them to sittonspelling@epsbooks.com or call 888-WE-SPELL for more assistance.

A Note from the Author

Dear Teachers,

Now you have an alternative to word-list spelling!

Yes, it's a *different* approach. The focus is on *strategies, not short-term memorization.* If you believe that good spellers are made, not born, then let's get started using what you learned in the seminar today. If nothing changes, nothing changes!

You'll see that your spelling and word-skill work is related to the experiences you're giving students in reading. Reading consists of decoding strategies and comprehension skills. *The goal of all reading instruction is to guide students to construct meaning from the words they've learned to read—so the words become useful as a reader.*

These reading skills are revisited in the form of encoding strategies in this methodology. Then, when students explore the rules that govern the spelling of a basic core of high-frequency writing words, they apply these skills to hundreds of words that serve to expand their vocabularies and word understandings. *The goal of all spelling instruction is to guide students to construct meaning from the words they've learned to spell—so the words become useful as a writer.*

Spelling and reading truly form a mutually beneficial tie—*if properly taught.* But watch out. Spelling—aligned with reading—is *not* creating a *spelling word list* from the words in a reading program's story. Any word-list approach to spelling does not prepare students for writing. Students only learn the words for the test, a short-term goal. Later, when students write, their memories fail them. No transfer!

It's time to move beyond excuses for students' poor spelling—it's not in the water! This research-based approach to spelling and word-skill literacy has the evidence to show it works! Let's work together to make every child a speller and a wordsmith!

P.S. Have you signed up for *Appleseed*, the complimentary e-newsletter of teaching ideas? Click on Appleseed at www.sittonspelling.com.

SEMINAR
EXTENSIONS

Word Bank of 1200 High-Frequency Core Words

the	1	into	61	another	121	few	181
of	2	has	62	came	122	those	182
and	3	more	63	come	123	always	183
a	4	her	64	work	124	show	184
to	5	two	65	three	125	large	185
in	6	like	66	must	126	often	186
is	7	him	67	because	127	together	187
you	8	see	68	does	128	asked	188
that	9	time	69	part	129	house	189
it	10	could	70	even	130	don't	190
he	11	no	71	place	131	world	191
for	12	make	72	well	132	going	192
was	13	than	73	such	133	want	193
on	14	first	74	here	134	school	194
are	15	been	75	take	135	important	195
as	16	its	76	why	136	until	196
with	17	who	77	help	137	form	197
his	18	now	78	put	138	food	198
they	19	people	79	different	139	keep	199
at	20	my	80	away	140	children	200
be	21	made	81	again	141	feet	201
this	22	over	82	off	142	land	202
from	23	did	83	went	143	side	203
I	24	down	84	old	144	without	204
have	25	only	85	number	145	boy	205
or	26	way	86	great	146	once	206
by	27	find	87	tell	147	animal	207
one	28	use	88	men	148	life	208
had	29	may	89	say	149	enough	209
not	30	water	90	small	150	took	210
but	31	long	91	every	151	four	211
what	32	little	92	found	152	head	212
all	33	very	93	still	153	above	213
were	34	after	94	between	154	kind	214
when	35	words	95	name	155	began	215
we	36	called	96	should	156	almost	216
there	37	just	97	home	157	live	217
can	38	where	98	big	158	page	218
an	39	most	99	give	159	got	219
your	40	know	100	air	160	earth	220
which	41	get	101	line	161	need	221
their	42	through	102	set	162	far	222
said	43	back	103	own	163	hand	223
if	44	much	104	under	164	high	224
do	45	go	105	read	165	year	225
will	46	good	106	last	166	mother	226
each	47	new	107	never	167	light	227
about	48	write	108	us	168	country	228
how	49	our	109	left	169	father	229
up	50	me	110	end	170	let	230
out	51	man	111	along	171	night	231
them	52	too	112	while	172	picture	232
then	53	any	113	might	173	being	233
she	54	day	114	next	174	study	234
many	55	same	115	sound	175	second	235
some	56	right	116	below	176	soon	236
so	57	look	117	saw	177	story	237
these	58	think	118	something	178	since	238
would	59	also	119	thought	179	white	239
other	60	around	120	both	180	ever	240

Sitton Spelling and Word Skills®

Word Bank of 1200 High-Frequency Core Words

paper	241	living	301	special	361	power	421
hard	242	black	302	ran	362	problem	422
near	243	eat	303	full	363	longer	423
sentence	244	short	304	town	364	winter	424
better	245	United States	305	complete	365	deep	425
best	246	run	306	oh	366	heavy	426
across	247	book	307	person	367	carefully	427
during	248	gave	308	hot	368	follow	428
today	249	order	309	anything	369	beautiful	429
however	250	open	310	hold	370	everyone	430
sure	251	ground	311	state	371	leave	431
knew	252	cold	312	list	372	everything	432
it's	253	really	313	stood	373	game	433
try	254	table	314	hundred	374	system	434
told	255	remember	315	ten	375	bring	435
young	256	tree	316	fast	376	watch	436
sun	257	course	317	felt	377	shell	437
thing	258	front	318	kept	378	dry	438
whole	259	American	319	notice	379	within	439
hear	260	space	320	can't	380	floor	440
example	261	inside	321	strong	381	ice	441
heard	262	ago	322	voice	382	ship	442
several	263	sad	323	probably	383	themselves	443
change	264	early	324	area	384	begin	444
answer	265	I'll	325	horse	385	fact	445
room	266	learned	326	matter	386	third	446
sea	267	brought	327	stand	387	quite	447
against	268	close	328	box	388	carry	448
top	269	nothing	329	start	389	distance	449
turned	270	though	330	that's	390	although	450
learn	271	idea	331	class	391	sat	451
point	272	before	332	piece	392	possible	452
city	273	lived	333	surface	393	heart	453
play	274	became	334	river	394	real	454
toward	275	add	335	common	395	simple	455
five	276	become	336	stop	396	snow	456
himself	277	grow	337	am	397	rain	457
usually	278	draw	338	talk	398	suddenly	458
money	279	yet	339	whether	399	easy	459
seen	280	less	340	fine	400	leaves	460
didn't	281	wind	341	round	401	lay	461
car	282	behind	342	dark	402	size	462
morning	283	cannot	343	past	403	wild	463
I'm	284	letter	344	ball	404	weather	464
body	285	among	345	girl	405	miss	465
upon	286	able	346	road	406	pattern	466
family	287	dog	347	blue	407	sky	467
later	288	shown	348	instead	408	walked	468
turn	289	mean	349	either	409	main	469
move	290	English	350	held	410	someone	470
face	291	rest	351	already	411	center	471
door	292	perhaps	352	warm	412	field	472
cut	293	certain	353	gone	413	stay	473
done	294	six	354	finally	414	itself	474
group	295	feel	355	summer	415	boat	475
true	296	fire	356	understand	416	question	476
half	297	ready	357	moon	417	wide	477
red	298	green	358	animals	418	least	478
fish	299	yes	359	mind	419	tiny	479
plants	300	built	360	outside	420	hour	480

Sitton Spelling and Word Skills®

Word Bank of 1200 High-Frequency Core Words

happened	481	bright	541	shape	601	various	661
foot	482	sent	542	eight	602	race	662
care	483	present	543	edge	603	bit	663
low	484	plan	544	soft	604	result	664
else	485	rather	545	village	605	brother	665
gold	486	length	546	object	606	addition	666
build	487	speed	547	age	607	doesn't	667
glass	488	machine	548	minute	608	dead	668
rock	489	information	549	wall	609	weight	669
tall	490	except	550	meet	610	thin	670
alone	491	figure	551	record	611	stone	671
bottom	492	you're	552	copy	612	hit	672
check	493	free	553	forest	613	wife	673
reading	494	fell	554	especially	614	island	674
fall	495	suppose	555	necessary	615	we'll	675
poor	496	natural	556	he's	616	opposite	676
map	497	ocean	557	unit	617	born	677
friend	498	government	558	flat	618	sense	678
language	499	baby	559	direction	619	cattle	679
job	500	grass	560	south	620	million	680
music	501	plane	561	subject	621	anyone	681
buy	502	street	562	skin	622	rule	682
window	503	couldn't	563	wasn't	623	science	683
mark	504	reason	564	I've	624	afraid	684
heat	505	difference	565	yellow	625	women	685
grew	506	maybe	566	party	626	produce	686
listen	507	history	567	force	627	pull	687
ask	508	mouth	568	test	628	son	688
single	509	middle	569	bad	629	meant	689
clear	510	step	570	temperature	630	broken	690
energy	511	child	571	pair	631	interest	691
week	512	strange	572	ahead	632	chance	692
explain	513	wish	573	wrong	633	thick	693
lost	514	soil	574	practice	634	sight	694
spring	515	human	575	sand	635	pretty	695
travel	516	trip	576	tail	636	train	696
wrote	517	woman	577	wait	637	fresh	697
farm	518	eye	578	difficult	638	drive	698
circle	519	milk	579	general	639	lead	699
whose	520	choose	580	cover	640	break	700
correct	521	north	581	material	641	sit	701
bed	522	seven	582	isn't	642	bought	702
measure	523	famous	583	thousand	643	radio	703
straight	524	late	584	sign	644	method	704
base	525	pay	585	guess	645	king	705
mountain	526	sleep	586	forward	646	similar	706
caught	527	iron	587	huge	647	return	707
hair	528	trouble	588	ride	648	corn	708
bird	529	store	589	region	649	decide	709
wood	530	beside	590	nor	650	position	710
color	531	oil	591	period	651	bear	711
war	532	modern	592	blood	652	hope	712
fly	533	fun	593	rich	653	song	713
yourself	534	catch	594	team	654	engine	714
seem	535	business	595	corner	655	board	715
thus	536	reach	596	cat	656	control	716
square	537	lot	597	amount	657	spread	717
moment	538	won't	598	garden	658	evening	718
teacher	539	case	599	led	659	brown	719
happy	540	speak	600	note	660	clean	720

Word Bank of 1200 High-Frequency Core Words

wouldn't	721	visit	781	separate	841	divide	901
section	722	sheep	782	truck	842	supply	902
spent	723	I'd	783	sing	843	laid	903
ring	724	office	784	column	844	dear	904
teeth	725	row	785	twice	845	surprise	905
quiet	726	contain	786	particular	846	gun	906
ancient	727	fit	787	shop	847	entire	907
stick	728	equal	788	unless	848	fruit	908
afternoon	729	value	789	spot	849	crowd	909
silver	730	yard	790	neither	850	band	910
nose	731	beat	791	met	851	wet	911
century	732	inch	792	wheel	852	solid	912
therefore	733	sugar	793	none	853	northern	913
level	734	key	794	hill	854	flower	914
you'll	735	product	795	television	855	star	915
death	736	desert	796	bill	856	feed	916
hole	737	bank	797	solve	857	wooden	917
coast	738	farther	798	pressure	858	sort	918
cross	739	won	799	report	859	develop	919
sharp	740	total	800	farmer	860	shoulder	920
fight	741	sell	801	count	861	variety	921
capital	742	wire	802	trade	862	season	922
fill	743	rose	803	chief	863	share	923
deal	744	cotton	804	month	864	jump	924
busy	745	spoke	805	clothes	865	regular	925
beyond	746	rope	806	doctor	866	represent	926
send	747	fear	807	indeed	867	market	927
love	748	shore	808	dance	868	we're	928
cool	749	throughout	809	church	869	flew	929
cause	750	compare	810	original	870	finger	930
please	751	movement	811	enjoy	871	expect	931
meat	752	exercise	812	string	872	army	932
lady	753	bread	813	sister	873	cabin	933
west	754	process	814	onto	875	camp	934
glad	755	nature	815	familiar	875	danger	935
action	756	apart	816	imagine	876	purpose	936
pass	757	path	817	blow	877	breakfast	937
type	758	careful	818	quick	878	proper	938
attention	759	narrow	819	law	879	coat	939
gas	760	mental	820	lie	880	push	940
kitchen	761	nine	821	final	881	express	941
pick	762	useful	822	rise	882	shot	942
scale	763	public	823	loud	883	angry	943
basic	764	according	824	fair	884	southern	944
happen	765	steel	825	herself	885	dress	945
safe	766	salt	826	slow	886	bag	946
grown	767	speech	827	noise	887	proud	947
cost	768	forth	828	statement	888	neck	948
wear	769	nation	829	hungry	889	breath	949
act	770	knowledge	830	join	890	strength	950
hat	771	appear	831	tube	891	member	951
arm	772	ate	832	rode	892	twelve	952
believe	773	dinner	833	empty	893	mine	953
major	774	hurt	834	twenty	894	company	954
gray	775	spend	835	broke	895	current	955
wonder	776	experiment	836	nice	896	pound	956
include	777	touch	837	effect	897	valley	957
describe	778	drop	838	paid	898	double	958
electric	779	chair	839	motion	899	till	959
sold	780	east	840	myself	900	match	960

Word Bank of 1200 High-Frequency Core Words

average	961	design	1021	muscles	1081	leather	1141
die	962	president	1022	model	1082	husband	1142
liquid	963	charge	1023	climate	1083	principal	1143
alive	964	mistake	1024	coffee	1084	medicine	1144
stream	965	hospital	1025	whenever	1085	excellent	1145
provide	966	remain	1026	serious	1086	operation	1146
drink	967	service	1027	angle	1087	council	1147
experience	968	increase	1028	feather	1088	author	1148
future	969	students	1029	determined	1089	organize	1149
tomorrow	970	insects	1030	dictionary	1090	concern	1150
drove	971	address	1031	ordinary	1091	barbecue	1151
population	972	sincerely	1032	extra	1092	accident	1152
finish	973	dollars	1033	rough	1093	disease	1153
station	974	belong	1034	library	1094	construction	1154
shook	975	bottle	1035	condition	1095	motor	1155
stage	976	flight	1036	arrived	1096	affect	1156
oxygen	977	forget	1037	located	1097	conversation	1157
poem	978	bicycle	1038	program	1098	evidence	1158
solution	979	secret	1039	pencil	1099	citizen	1159
burn	980	soldier	1040	tongue	1100	environment	1160
cent	981	silent	1041	title	1101	influence	1161
electricity	982	structure	1042	enemy	1102	cancel	1162
everybody	983	height	1043	garage	1103	audience	1163
rate	984	observe	1044	lose	1104	apartment	1164
dust	985	indicate	1045	vegetable	1105	worse	1165
worth	986	railroad	1046	parents	1106	transportation	1166
community	987	knife	1047	style	1107	frozen	1167
captain	988	married	1048	education	1108	waste	1168
bus	989	suggested	1049	required	1109	couple	1169
protect	990	entered	1050	political	1110	function	1170
cook	991	magazine	1051	daughter	1111	connect	1171
raise	992	agree	1052	individual	1112	project	1172
further	993	fifty	1053	progress	1113	pronounce	1173
steam	994	escape	1054	altogether	1114	offered	1174
guide	995	threw	1055	activities	1115	apply	1175
discover	996	planet	1056	article	1116	improve	1176
plain	997	dangerous	1057	equipment	1117	stomach	1177
usual	998	event	1058	discuss	1118	collect	1178
seat	999	leader	1059	healthy	1119	prevent	1179
accept	1000	peace	1060	perfect	1120	courage	1180
police	1001	spelling	1061	recognize	1121	occur	1181
consider	1002	chapter	1062	frequently	1122	foreign	1182
dozen	1003	swimming	1063	character	1123	quality	1183
baseball	1004	opportunity	1064	personal	1124	terrible	1184
rubber	1005	immediately	1065	disappear	1125	instrument	1185
symbol	1006	favorite	1066	success	1126	balance	1186
support	1007	settled	1067	traffic	1127	ability	1187
exactly	1008	telephone	1068	yesterday	1128	arrange	1188
industry	1009	repeat	1069	situation	1129	rhythm	1189
they're	1010	prepare	1070	realize	1130	avoid	1190
beneath	1011	instance	1071	message	1131	daily	1191
laugh	1012	avenue	1072	recently	1132	identity	1192
groceries	1013	newspaper	1073	account	1133	standard	1193
popular	1014	actually	1074	physical	1134	combine	1194
thank	1015	employee	1075	neighbor	1135	attached	1195
quarter	1016	review	1076	excited	1136	frighten	1196
climbed	1017	convince	1076	whisper	1137	social	1197
continue	1018	allowed	1078	available	1138	factory	1198
potatoes	1019	nobody	1079	college	1139	license	1199
receive	1020	details	1080	furniture	1140	recommend	1200

Core Words are high-frequency writing words 1–1200, introduced in order of frequency of use. They are divided by grade level 1–8 and are used in each grade from which to springboard to grow essential skills and concepts. The skill- and concept-building activities that grow from a single Core Word generate many more words, so that students have word experiences that extend their grade-level Core Words to hundreds of words and new understandings about their language.

See pages 38–42 for a complete list of Core Words in order of frequency in writing.
See page 10 for grade-specific divisions of Core Words for teaching skills and concepts.
See student Practice Books for grade-specific lists of Core Words for student reference.

Spelling Words are Core Words that are misspelled or misused on a Cloze Story Word Test and/or the Sentence Dictation Test in each unit. The bank of words from which the test words are taken is every previously introduced Core Word, beginning with word 1 (*the*), up to the current unit in which students are being tested. An alphabetized list for each grade is on a blackline master in the appropriate Sourcebook, and can be sent home at the beginning of the school year.

See pages 66–68 for an explanation of the tests.
See page 29 for grade-specific divisions of potential Core Words for testing.

Priority Words are Core Words that are designated as "no excuses" words and cannot be missed in writing—ever! These words begin with *the* in first grade, and grow to about 130 by the end of grade eight—and it is within this bank of the highest-use words that most spelling errors are made, even among college-educated adults. As students write, they may refer to these words. The Priority Words are alphabetized on a blackline master for each grade in the appropriate Sourcebook, and can be noted with a highlighter as they become Priority Words over time. Some teachers prefer to identify Priority Words on My Spell Check® (grades 1–2) or Spell Check® (grades 3–8).

See pages 69–72 for an explanation for using Priority Words.
See page 31 for grade-specific expectations for Priority Words.
See page 163 for information on My Spell Check/Spell Check cards.
See student Practice Books for grade-specific list of Priority Words for student reference.

Topical Words are words for which students have been given a reference to use while they write on a particular topic, often a content-area everyday writing piece. They are Priority Words, but for a limited time—perhaps for just one assignment.

See top of page 70.

Everyday Writing is daily writing that is writing completed in subjects across the curriculum. It is not writing that is part of the Writing Process, papers revised over time to create an error-free final copy.

The purpose of the Word Preview is to teach and practice a visual strategy. It is a powerful procedure to diminish careless errors among known words in writing. Every teacher's dilemma is how to get students to proofread for these misspellings! A step toward this end that is often overlooked is straightforward, teacher-directed instruction on visual skills so that students learn *how to proofread*. This overt instruction can be achieved best through the Word Preview.

Then as students apply these essential visual skills practiced in the Word Preview, they are able to proofread for words, many of which they are able to spell, but have misspelled in their writing because their thoughts are on content and not on spelling. Further, when the effort becomes a habit, students' written communication skills are enhanced.

In addition to everyday spelling and writing benefits, the skills the Word Preview targets are those skills necessary for improved test scores on standardized and performance-based spelling tests. These tests are proofreading and/or editing tests.

The Word Preview and a pretest in a customary program may be perceived as the same. They are not. The research indicates that a pretest was never meant to be a test. The name "test" has created misconceptions that undermine its effectiveness. For example, words spelled correctly on a pretest are considered "mastered" and are not signaled for further study. Yet, every teacher experiences frustration when students who spell words correctly on a pretest, or a customary Friday post test, are unable to spell the same words in everyday writing! Indeed, if this procedure is perceived as a test, it yields invalid assessment information that results in false assumptions that compromise the integrity of the spelling curriculum.

The words used for this procedure are called Core Words. They are not the Spelling Words. Core Words are high-frequency words assigned to each grade level for the purpose of teaching skills. In the Word Preview, the Core Words teach visual skills. There are five Core Words for each Word Preview for grades 2–8, and three words for grade 1.

Students *do not prestudy* the Core Words for the Word Preview. It is not a test of short-term memory of words recently studied.

The research-based steps for administering the Word Preview need to be followed carefully to get the best results. Tell students what you expect. Give all the words, then spell the first word for students to self-check. Next, write the first word on the chalkboard for students to rewrite. Follow this model with each word sequentially.

Remind students as they check their words for errors to circle only the part of the word they missed—not the whole word. This helps students see that only part of the word is wrong. Also, be certain that students do not write the word in the rewrite column during step 4 while you write the word on the chalkboard and say the name of each letter. Students should rewrite each word in the rewrite column without the advantage of hearing you say the name of each letter.

After the Word Preview, you or an assistant should examine, but not grade, each student's rewrite column for spelling accuracy. Have students fold their first attempt to write the words (the write column) to the back so that it cannot be seen. Do not look at this column. Checking these words may encourage some students to fix their first attempt to write the words, making it appear that they spelled them correctly on the first try. If this activity surfaces, ignore it. With your attention solely on the rewrite column, students abandon their unproductive "fixing" activity.

When students are familiar with the procedure, the Word Preview should take less than five minutes. Maintain a fast, but comfortable pace. Students learn to listen and write the words quickly and confidently. To encourage this, do not repeat words.

If a word is misspelled in the rewrite column, make a small dot next to it to indicate the mistake. Errors should be corrected by the students, not you.

For students who are absent for the Word Preview, a make-up Word Preview can be given by you or an assistant, such as a teacher's aide, student, or parent volunteer. In lieu of giving a make-up Word Preview, the student who missed the Word Preview could preview the Core Words by using the Word Study Strategy.

There are other visual skill-building exercises that complement this routine, such as the Word Study Strategy. Further, there is a selection of visual activities included in the section of the Sourcebook Series labeled Seeds for Sowing Skills. For still more activities, see Developing Visual Skills in this handbook.

For students who have not developed the ability to copy a word from the chalkboard, see Students With Spelling Challenges in this handbook. If the procedure appears too easy for some students, remember that its purpose is to provide practice visualizing known words and to check students' ability to copy and proofread them. It is not a procedure to challenge spelling ability, so do not add words with the intention of increasing rigor. This would diminish effectiveness.

If students are able to spell, copy, and proofread each of the Core Words on the Word Preview, this is not confirmation that they have mastered them. The Core Words on the Word Preview are not a student's spelling list. Instead, the Core Words used in the Word Preview are simply words used to develop visual skills, and then many other skills as the unit progresses to make every child a speller.

The Word Preview is <u>different</u> from the pretest in—

1. Name

    Its name, the Word Preview, represents its intended use.

2. Purpose

    Its use as a visual skill-building practice activity reflects the intent of the research, while its use as a test does not reflect the research and serves to provide inaccurate information on word mastery.

3. Number of words

    A less time-consuming procedure contributes to easier use.

4. Time frame

    Flexibility is increased when the procedure can be given on any day, and takes no more than five minutes.

5. Words

    The words on the Word Preview are <u>not</u> the Spelling Words for the unit.

MORE WAYS TO
DEVELOP THE
VISUAL SKILLS

Visual skills needed for spelling are different from those needed for reading. The former requires careful attention to individual letters, while the latter requires the reader to focus on phrases. Well-developed visual skills are essential to learn to spell (visualizing the correct letters in words) and to apply proofreading skills once words have been written. Clearly, learning to spell words and proofreading written work are of equal importance in moving students to the goal of being literate writers.

This program addresses the development of visual skills in several ways. First, the Word Preview that introduces each unit is a highly effective procedure to develop visual skills—a strategy to see each sequential letter in a word. It follows the real intent of research, a method of teaching students to see individual letters—not a spelling test. Second, the Word Study Strategy is an effective, researched method to complement the Word Preview. Students can use this strategy in class, and parents can use it to help their children at home. Third, visual skill-building is reinforced in the activities included in the skills lessons.

Visual skills can be taught and learned. Students benefit from general visual skill-building activities even as they are participating in the procedures described above. Following are visual skill-building ideas for your review.

Activities to Recall and Develop Images

Developing Immediate Recall
Show students the cover of a book, a simple picture, common objects in a box, or ask students to observe a classmate. Allow thirty seconds for observation. Remove the object(s) or have the classmate step outside the room and ask students to write, discuss, or draw details they remember. Show the object(s) or observe the classmate again and compare the accuracy of their descriptions.

Developing Recall of Familiar Objects
Ask students to recall the details of familiar things they have seen in the past. For instance, ask students to create a mind picture of the school office, the principal, their kitchen at home, a paper clip, or a familiar object they often use or see. Have students write, discuss, or draw the details remembered. Then compare the mental images with the actual thing.

Place a few familiar objects in a dark plastic garbage bag and tape it shut. Ask students to feel the objects and try to identify them. Next, have the students tell or write what they think is inside the bag. Check the contents of the bag to confirm their answers.

Show students a shape or design drawn on a large card. Ask students to study it and create a mental picture of it. Then have them draw what they recall seeing. Begin with easy shapes and designs, such as a circle with an x inside. Progress to more complex formations. Then include high-use writing words.

Developing Visual Images Through Grid-Paper Games

Word-Shape Exercises

Students write current or review Core Words (particularly their Spelling Words) in the boxes using grid paper. They extend the tall letters into the boxes above the base of the word, and tail letters extend into the boxes below the base word. Then students outline the word's shape. Another approach is to predraw the word shapes on grid paper. Students find and write the appropriate word, recall the word, and write it again. You may wish to draw a word-shape game on the chalkboard. Students write and outline words on their grid paper that match that shape. This game can be played among individual players or in teams.

Crossword and Word-Search Puzzles

Grid activities include crossword puzzles and word-search games. The words in Word Search games should be written left-to-right or top-to-bottom, or on the left-to-right diagonal. Students prepare games for classmates to complete.

Discovering Hidden Words to Promote Visual Ability

Exercises that help students identify specific words among many letters are motivational and productive. Students can complete the activities as well as make them for classmates to complete. As a follow-up activity, ask students to write the game words. Have them turn their paper over, call the words up in their mind's eye, and write the words again.

Words-in-Words Game

Have students find and write words they find inside of words. This can be played in two versions. One way is to specify that the actual word is written inside of another word, such as *he*, *her*, *the*, and *here* inside of *there*. In another version, students write words using letters from a given word, such as *hat* and *tan* from *than*.

Be a Word Detective

Within a sequence of random letters, students circle and write words that are hiding among the letters. For example, students write *try* and *or* from this sequence of letters: *dftyorsktry*.

Word Scramble

The best scrambles are those in which the scrambled letters "float" inside of a cloud or other shape so that the scrambled word is not confused with an actual word.

Enhancing Visual Discrimination

Same Words Game

Write a row of similar words on the chalkboard or blackline master. Students find and circle a given word. For example:

   sheep: street sheep sleep sheet cheap cheat stream sheep steep sheet

Look-Alike Word Maker

Write game words on the chalkboard or on a blackline master. Students use all letters of each game word to make another word. For example, students would make *mean* from *name*.

Write and Erase

Write a word on the chalkboard, let students look at it for a few seconds, and then erase it. Students should look at the board and try to visualize the word still being there. Next, students write the word on their paper or personal chalkboard.

EXERCISE EXPRESS

In the seminar, you engaged in Exercise Express lessons featured in each unit of the Sourcebook Series. Here is an explanation of these quick practice ideas that develop spelling and language-related skills at school or at home. They can be independently completed, a cooperative group activity, a paired student lesson, or a teacher-directed activity. First, model the activities, as well as suggest appropriate responses. Modeling suggestions are in each grade-level Sourcebook Teaching Notes for Exercise Express.

STRETCH IT
ADD WORDS TO MAKE THIS SENTENCE LONGER AND BETTER

Provide a sentence to students. Ask them to add words to expand the sentence.
The foremost goal of Stretch It is to increase students' level of writing sophistication by providing instruction and practice on sentence expansion. Students learn how to take a "bare bones" sentence and embellish it to make it more informative and interesting. Further, students practice writing, spelling, and proofreading.

FIX IT
THIS SENTENCE IS NOT RIGHT. FIX IT.

Provide a sentence to students that contains proofreading errors. Ask students to proofread the sentence and identify the errors. Then they rewrite the sentence correctly.
Fix It provides instruction and practice on editing and proof-reading. This benefits students' everyday writing. It also prepares students for performance on standardized and/or state and district spelling tests, which assess editing and proofreading skills. As students have more experience with these tasks, you can expect better performance on the tests. At first, you may wish to tell students how many errors to find. Later, expect students to find all the errors without this aid. The errors for revision can include spelling, homophone usage, capitalization, punctuation, grammar—increasing in difficulty as students progress. A classroom "Fix It" chart could guide students during this activity. The chart could remind students to check every letter of every word, homophones, capitals, punctuation, and grammar.

FIND IT
FIND AND WRITE THE WORDS

Provide students with a criterion for finding words. Then ask students to list words that reflect the criterion.
Find It expands students' word experiences to help them become discriminating observers of words. It offers an opportunity to search for, write, and proofread words.

Provide students with words for sorting. Ask students to sort the words in some way. Then students explain how they sorted the words.

Sort It helps students compare and contrast words—to think about their commonalities and differences. This powerful means of exploring words develops skills, including vocabulary, visual, phonemic awareness, structural analysis, and phonetic analysis. A sorting exercise can use a closed or open format. In closed sorts, students are told the categories into which the words are sorted. In open sorts, students examine the words and determine their own categories. At first, use the closed format for the word sorts. In time, use the more difficult open sorts.

Provide students with a set of words that reflect a commonality or sequence. Then ask students to provide more words that reflect the criterion.

Add It is an analytical activity to teach students to examine a bank of words to discover a commonality and/or pattern among them. Add It is one more way for students to work with and think about words. A classroom "Add It" chart could guide students during this activity (optional teacher-made chart). After the first lesson, the chart could list "same spelling pattern." Then the chart could grow as new commonalities are discovered in subsequent Add It lessons.

Provide students with a sentence or partial sentence. Ask them to finish the sentence, perhaps developing it into a paragraph or story.

Finish It activities provide practice in thinking, writing, spelling, and proofreading. It is an invitation for students to use their imagination to create a conclusion to an open-ended idea. Then they write about it and proofread their work. Sentence and/or story starters are efficient ways to encourage these skills, particularly among reluctant writers. A classroom "Finish It" chart could guide students during this activity. Guide words could include: Who, What, Where, When, Why, How, Size, and Color.

Provide students with a key word. Then have students list synonyms to strengthen their word bank.

Replace It is a word-building activity in Exercise Express at Levels 7 and 8. The greater students' word banks, the greater their capacity to think, speak, spell, and write.

During the seminar, skill-building activities were demonstrated. These activities were selected from among the menu of activity ideas in the Seeds for Sowing Skills section of each unit in the Sourcebook Series. The purpose of the activities is to provide students a foundation in basic skills and concepts, enabling them to build spelling and related language understandings that they can apply to the spelling of hundreds of additional words. The purpose of the activities is *not to teach specific words*, but to provide students with opportunities to explore words to make generalizations about them that enable them to become independent, strategic spellers—not for a Friday Test, but forever.

The skills and concepts are developed through activities that grow from the Core Words. Core Words are high-frequency words assigned to each grade level that are used to teach skills. Again, mastering the spelling of the Core Words is *not the purpose* of these skill- and concept-building activities.

The skills and concepts are best developed in active, not passive formats. They can be developed as paired or small group activities, whole-class teacher-directed lessons, homework, independent exercises—or any combination of these elements. For teachers who choose to use the Practice Books for Learning Spelling and Words Skills (see page 161), students become engaged in recording their word collections, analyzing them, generalizing, and expanding their understanding of their language and how it works.

All skills and concepts need recycling. Recycling skills has benefits. First, ongoing exposure and reinforcement aids long-term learning. Another benefit of recycling is the opportunity it provides for differentiating instruction. Initially some skills or concepts may be too difficult to present to all or some students. Over time, these same skills and concepts may become too easy for most students, but be on target for other students— hence, differentiated instruction.

Further, recycling makes teaching for mastery unnecessary. Mastery grows over time. So, if students initially have difficulty with a skill or concept, move on because subsequent exposures will afford students the desired mastery. Finally, when skills and concepts recur routinely, they offer ongoing opportunities for informal measurement of students' progress and mastery. This empowers you to make informed decisions on the selection of subsequent skill-building activities to meet your students' specific needs.

FOR YOUR INFORMATION

YOU CHOOSE THE SEEDS TO SOW AND GROW A GARDEN OF ABLE SPELLERS!

The seeds have been sown. Now for the harvest! <u>What are the benefits?</u>

1. Basic skills and concepts

    Benefit: Skills and concepts are restored! This increases teaching effectiveness and learning outcomes, because it is easier to help students discover a few well-chosen, research-based generalizations that can be applied to many words, than to teach "lists" of words, each one learned as a separate set of letters.

2. Spelling logic

    Benefit: Students develop a foundation for learning to think about words. They become discriminating observers of words—their spellings, meanings, and use.

3. More words

    Benefit: The activities develop hundreds of words beyond the words listed in a customary spelling unit. Research indicates that the more word experiences students have, the better prepared they are to think, speak, spell, read, and write.

4. Students' involvement

    Benefit: Research on learning verifies that student involvement increases learning. The unit activities provide multiple opportunities for student involvement, as the teacher assumes the role of "facilitator."

5. Parent-child partnerships

    Benefit: Studies of exemplary educational programs clearly provide evidence that parent involvement enhances student progress. Parent opportunities abound in this methodology, particularly with skill exercises—see "Parents as Partners."

6. Flexibility

    Benefit: Opportunities for customized instruction and differentiated practice within any time frame is achieved through teachers' self-selection of activities from a wide menu of choices making teaching and learning easier and more effective.

7. A balanced program

    Benefit: With extensive choices for skill-building, teachers can provide balance to a total communications curriculum—even as adopted reading and language materials change over time.

8. Increased test scores

    Benefit: Students who understand the skills that govern spelling—those skills and concepts taught in this methodology—are better prepared to take spelling and word-skill achievement tests.

9. Writing fluency

    Benefit: Students who have the words and skills for writing find it easier to write and often assume lead roles as adults in positions that require writing literacy.

Sitton Spelling and Word Skills®
3rd edition

Skills and Concepts for Grade 1

Formal spelling instruction can begin when first graders can read, know the names of the letters and can write them, know that letters make words, and have acquired a phonological awareness. They have participated in guided writing, predicting spellings as words are written, and are emerging as writers through attempting the spelling of words through approximations.

A first grader's spelling experiences should include:
- **spelling by analogy** (onsets and rimes: _at—sat, bat, hat)
- **short vowel spelling patterns** (words with one vowel: not)
- **long vowel spelling patterns** (words with two vowels: note)
- **consonant spelling patterns** (/z/: boxes, was, wise, zip, fuzzy)
- **spelling digraphs** (ch/chin, sh/wish, th/this, wh/when)
- **spelling double-letter words** (will)
- **words spelled the way they sound** (that)
- **words not spelled the way they sound** (they)
- **silent letters** (have)
- **predicting spellings in guided writing**
- **spelling consonant blends** (from, stop, plan)
- **consonant and vowel letter substitutions** (letter-card manipulations)

Further, students should learn **strategies** that enable them to anticipate the spelling of a word, such as:
- a short vowel sound is usually spelled with one vowel.
- double letters stand for one sound.
- knowing how to spell one word may help spell rhyming words.
- some letters spell more than one sound.

Spelling experiences should be integrated with opportunities for **language growth**, such as **antonyms** (in/out), **homophones** (for/four), **regular plurals** (cats), **contractions** (that's), **multiple meanings** (can), **idioms** (to have a fit, to have a ball, to have the blues), **sorting words** (by phonic properties, structural attributes), **vocabulary development** through the discussion of unfamiliar words, such as those generated in patterning activities (man, tan, ban), making words through the addition of **suffixes** (s, ed, ing).

Experiences with literature should be plentiful, learning the concept of story and the use of words in context to write one.

Explicit instruction in **visual skills** is essential, including the Word Preview—then students apply these skills in writing and proofreading.

Students need abundant **writing opportunities** (guided, structured, dictated, independent) to work toward the mastery of **Core Words** 1–35, to grow them into many more words, and to maintain 100% accuracy in all everyday writing for **Priority Words** 1–15 (by the end of the school year).

Sitton Spelling and Word Skills®

3rd edition

Level 2

Skills and Concepts for Grade 2

A second grader's spelling experiences should include:

- **spelling by analogy** (onsets and rimes: _ill—bill, fill, hill)
- **short vowel spelling patterns** (words with one vowel: him)
- **long vowel spelling patterns** (long a: make, day, rain)
- **consonant spelling patterns** (/k/: came, kite, back, question, school)
- **spelling digraphs** (ch/much, sh/should, th/another, wh/which)
- **spelling double-letter words** (off, still, glass)
- **irregular spellings** (many, does, great, said)
- **silent letters** (would, people, know, like)
- *r*-**controlled vowels** (more, her, first, part)
- **predicting spellings in guided writing**
- **spelling consonant blends** (clap, stem, brush)
- **consonant and vowel letter substitutions** (letter-card manipulations)
- **introduction of possessive pronouns** (his, our, my)

Further, students should learn **strategies** that enable them to anticipate the spelling of a word, such as:

- long vowel words are often spelled with two vowels (like).
- /ou/ is consistently spelled *ou* (about) or *ow* (down).
- a long *i* or a long *e* sound at the end of a word is usually spelled *y* (why, many).

Spelling experiences should be integrated with opportunities for **language growth**, such as **antonyms** (down/up), **synonyms** (little, tiny), **homophones** (no/know), **homographs** (does, use, read), **regular** and **irregular plurals** (days, men, ladies, dishes), **contractions** (wouldn't, you're), **multiple meanings** (can, will), **idioms** (up and coming, up in arms), **sorting words** (by phonic properties, structural attributes, meaning), **compound words** (highway), **vocabulary development** through the discussion of unfamiliar words, such as those generated in patterning activities (way, play, *stray*).

Students should explore **other word forms** of high-use writing words through the addition of **prefixes** (re, un) and **suffixes** (s, ed, ing, es, er, est, ly, ful, y), and the **basic rules** that govern their use, such as the addition of suffixes to words in which the final consonant is doubled, the final silent *e* is dropped, the final *y* is changed to *i*, and the final letter is *s*, *x*, *sh*, *ch*, or *z*. Further, students should explore **irregular verb forms**.

Explicit instruction in **visual skills** is essential, including the Word Preview—then students apply these skills in writing and proofreading.

Students need abundant **writing opportunities** to work toward the mastery of **Core Words** 1–170, to grow them into many more words, and to maintain 100% accuracy in all everyday writing for **Priority Words** 1–35 (by the end of the school year).

Sitton Spelling and Word Skills®
3rd edition

Level 3

Skills and Concepts for Grade 3

A third grader's spelling experiences should include:

- **spelling by analogy** (_est: best, guest, quest)
- **short and long vowel spelling patterns** (long *a*: stay, train, space)
- **consonant spelling patterns** (/k/: came, kite, back, question, school)
- **soft/hard consonant spellings** (c: city, bicycle, once; second, American, cutting)
- **consonant blends** (_r: try, group, throne)
- **irregular spellings** (through, thought, great)
- **multisyllabic words** (together, important)
- **silent letters** (castle, write, take, bright, lamb)
- **spelling digraphs** (both, white, crash, children)
- **spelling diphthongs** (/ou/: sound, clown; /oi/: point, boy)
- **spelling double-letter words** (across, usually, beginning)
- **spelling vowel-*r*** (/or/: morning, before)
- **spelling soft-syllable endings** (/ər/: ever, color, dollar)
- **letter substitutions** (letter-card manipulations)

Further, students should learn **strategies** that enable them to anticipate the spelling of a word, such as when /k/ follows a short vowel, it is usually spelled *ck* (luck), and when /k/ does not follow a short vowel, it is usually spelled *k* or *ke* (bark, like). The *ke* spelling is signaled by a long vowel sound. Students learn that this concept also applies to /ch/ (lunch, catch) and /j/ (judge, large).

Spelling experiences should be integrated with opportunities for **language growth**, such as identifying and spelling **antonyms** (always/never), **synonyms** (large, huge, gigantic), **homophones** (there/their/they're), **homographs** (live, read, does), **possessives** (Dan's, student's, ours), **regular** and **irregular plurals** (hats, inches, ladies, children), **contractions** (couldn't), **compound words** (something), **multiple meanings** (feet), **idioms** (to change hands), **analogies** (came : come :: said : say), **sorting words** (by meaning, phonic properties, structural attributes).

Students should explore **other word forms** of high-use writing words through the addition of **prefixes** (re, un) and **suffixes** (s, ed, ing, es, er, est, ly, ful, y), and the **basic rules** that govern their use, such as the addition of suffixes to words in which the final consonant is doubled, the final silent *e* is dropped, the final *y* is changed to *i*, and the final letter is *s*, *x*, *sh*, *ch*, or *z*. Further, students should explore **irregular verb forms**.

Explicit instruction in **visual skills** is essential, including the Word Preview—then students apply these skills in writing and proofreading.

Students need abundant **writing opportunities** to work toward the mastery of **Core Words** 1–335, to grow them into many more words, and to maintain 100% accuracy in all everyday writing for **Priority Words** 1–55 (by the end of the school year).

Sitton Spelling and Word Skills®

3rd edition

Level 4

Skills and Concepts for Grade 4

A fourth grader's spelling experiences should include:

- **spelling by analogy** (be_: behind, became, behave)
- **short and long vowel spelling patterns** (long *a*: able, state, rainy, today)
- **consonant spelling patterns** (/j/: just, change, giant, gym)
- **hard/soft consonant spellings** (c: cities, fancy, notice; complete, carefully, cute)
- **consonant blends** (_r: library, hundred, scratch)
- **irregular spellings** (build, watch, friend)
- **multisyllabic words** (information)
- **silent letters** (become, often, walk, answer)
- **spelling digraphs** (weather, English, wheel, telephone, check)
- **spelling diphthongs** (/ou/: hour, power; /oi/: voice, enjoy)
- **spelling vowel-*r*** (/er/: certain, third, surface)
- **spelling soft-syllable endings** (/əl/: apple, final, camel)
- **letter substitutions** (letter-card manipulations)

Further, students should learn **strategies** that enable them to anticipate the spelling of a word, such as /er/ is usually spelled *er*, *ir*, or *ur* in stressed syllables (person, circle, surface), but when /er/ follows /w/, the sound is usually spelled *or* (world).

Spelling experiences should be integrated with opportunities for **language growth**, such as identifying and spelling **antonyms** (summer/winter), **synonyms** (construct, build), **homophones** (there/their/they're, there's/theirs), **homographs** (wound, object), **possessives** (Maria's, friend's, his), **regular** and **irregular plurals** (hearts, geese), **contractions** (shouldn't), **compound words** (everything), **multiple meanings** (check), **analogies** (common : uncommon :: complete : incomplete), **idioms** (caught short), the meaning and use of **often confused words** (lose/loose), **abbreviations** (hour/hr.), **sorting words** (by meaning, phonetic analysis, structural attributes), **Greek** and **Latin roots** (port/transport).

Students should explore **other word forms** of high-use writing words through the addition of **prefixes** (anti, de, dis, ex, im, in, mis, multi, re, sub, un) and **suffixes** (s, ed, ing, es, er, est, ly, ful, y, less, able, ty, ness, ment, ship, th, ion/sion/tion), and the **basic rules** that govern their use, such as the addition of suffixes to words in which the final consonant is doubled (including stressed final syllables), the final silent *e* is dropped, the final *y* is changed to *i*, and the final letter is *s*, *x*, *sh*, *ch*, or *z*. Further, students should explore **irregular verb forms.**

Explicit instruction in **visual skills** is essential, including the Word Preview—then students apply these skills in writing and proofreading.

Students need abundant **writing opportunities** to work toward the mastery of **Core Words** 1–500, to grow them into many more words, and to maintain 100% accuracy in all everyday writing for **Priority Words** 1–75 (by the end of the school year).

Sitton Spelling and Word Skills®

3rd edition

Skills and Concepts for Grade 5

A fifth grader's spelling experiences should include:

- **spelling by analogy** (measure, pleasure, treasure)
- **short and long vowel spelling patterns** (long *a*: baby, race, straight, maybe)
- **consonant spelling patterns** (/j/: object, general, giraffe, gymnasium)
- **hard/soft consonant spellings** (c: circle, cyclone, necessary; copy, caught, difficult)
- **consonant blends** (str_: street, stretch, destroy)
- **irregular spellings** (whose, guess, island)
- **multisyllabic words** (especially)
- **silent letters** (listen, sign)
- **spelling digraphs** (brother, shape, whether, teacher, atmosphere)
- **spelling diphthongs** (/ou/: thousand, downhill; /oi/: soil, joyful)
- **spelling vowel-*r*** (/or/: forward, shore)
- **spelling soft-syllable endings** (/əl/: single, travel, natural; /ən(t)s/: difference, distance)
- **letter substitutions** (letter-card manipulations of longer words)

Further, students should learn **strategies** that enable them to anticipate the spelling of a word, such as the addition of a prefix never changes the spelling of the base word (mis + spelling = misspelling), but the addition of a suffix may change the spelling of a base word, particularly for words ending in silent *e*, one vowel and one consonant, or consonant-*y*.

Spelling experiences should be integrated with opportunities for **language growth**, such as identifying and spelling **antonyms** (reasonable/unreasonable), **synonyms** (maybe, possibly, perhaps), **homophones** (you're/your, its/it's, whose/who's), **homographs** (present), **idioms** (mark time), **possessives** (woman's, birds', yours), **regular** and **irregular plurals** (calves, deer), **contractions** (we'll), **compound words** (baseball), **multiple meanings** (check), **analogies** (woman : women :: party : parties), the meaning and use of **often-confused words** (cease/seize), **abbreviations** (mountain/mtn.), **sorting words** (by meaning, phonetic analysis, structural attributes), **Greek** and **Latin roots** (form/uniform).

Students should explore **other word forms** of high-use writing words through the addition of all common **prefixes** and **suffixes**, and the **basic rules** that govern their use. Further, students should explore **irregular verb forms**.

Explicit instruction in **visual skills** is essential, including the Word Preview—then students apply these skills in writing and proofreading.

Students need abundant **writing opportunities** to work toward the mastery of **Core Words** 1–675, to grow them into many more words, and to maintain 100% accuracy in all everyday writing for **Priority Words** 1–100 (by the end of the school year).

Sitton Spelling and Word Skills®

3rd edition

Level 6

Skills and Concepts for Grade 6

A sixth grader's spelling experiences should include:

- **spelling by analogy** (basic, electric, comic, athletic)
- **vowel spelling patterns** (review all previous patterns)
- **consonant spelling patterns and blends** (review all previous patterns)
- **irregular spellings** (break, neither, yacht, colonel)
- **silent letters** (column, bought, hymn)
- **spelling digraphs, diphthongs, and vowel-***r*** (review all previous patterns)
- **spelling soft-syllable endings** (ery/ary/ory/ury, ant/ent, ance/ence, able/ible)
- **challenging letter groups** (ie/ei: sleigh, believe; ou variants: cough)
- **challenging double-letter words** (disappoint, accurate, controlled)
- **foreign spellings** (French *ch* spelling /sh/: parachute, machine, chef)

Further, students should learn **strategies** that enable them to anticipate the spelling of a word, such as:

- for the addition of the *able* suffix to a word ending in silent *e*, drop the *e* unless the consonant letter before the silent *e* is *c* or *g* (lovable, noticeable, changeable).
- *s* usually spells /s/, but *sc* or *c* can spell /s/ before *e*, *i*, or *y*.
- when /j/ follows a short vowel, it is usually spelled *dge* (judge) and is usually spelled *ge* when it does not (large).

Spelling experiences should be integrated with opportunities for **language growth,** such as identifying and spelling **antonyms** (evening/dawn), **synonyms** (glad, elated, pleased), **homophones** (continued practice with the most misused sets; expansion to less familiar **homophones,** e.g., cereal/serial, board/bored), **homographs** (produce), **idioms** (born yesterday), **similes/metaphors** (as quiet as a mouse), **possessives** (theirs, Monty's, teachers', children's), **regular** and **irregular plurals** (cattle, teeth, *o*-ending words, shelves), **mispronounced words** (recognize, arctic), **contractions** (we'll), **compound words** (throughout, therefore), **multiple meanings** (interest), **analogies** (major : minor :: careful : careless), **often-confused words** (senses/census/consensus, desert/dessert), **abbreviations** (boulevard/blvd.), **sorting words** (by meaning, phonetic analysis, structural attributes), **Greek** and **Latin roots** (sci: science, conscience).

Students should explore **other word forms** of high-use writing words through the addition of all common **prefixes** and **suffixes,** and the **basic rules** that govern their use, particularly with **multisyllabic words.** Further, students should explore **irregular verb forms.**

Explicit instruction in **visual skills** is essential, including the Word Preview—then students apply these skills in writing and proofreading.

Students need abundant **writing opportunities** to work toward the mastery of **Core Words** 1–850, to grow them into many more words, and to maintain 100% accuracy in all everyday writing for **Priority Words** 1–130 (by the end of the school year).

Sitton Spelling and Word Skills®
3rd edition

Level 7

Skills and Concepts for Grade 7

A seventh grader's spelling experiences should include:
- **spelling by analogy** (breath, weather, leather)
- **vowel spelling patterns** (review all previous patterns)
- **consonant spelling patterns and blends** (review all previous patterns)
- **irregular spellings** (laugh, double, sergeant, vacuum)
- **silent letters** (design, plumber, wrinkle, guide)
- **spelling digraphs, diphthongs, and vowel-*r*** (review all previous patterns)
- **spelling soft-syllable endings** (ant/ent, ance/ence, able/ible, or/er/ar, al/el/le)
- **challenging letter groups** (ie/ei, ize/ise, ou)
- **challenging double-letter words** (tomorrow, community, hurricane)
- **foreign spellings** (French *eau* spells long *o*: bureau, plateau)

Further, students should learn **strategies** that enable them to anticipate the spelling of a word, such as:
- for the addition of the *ly* suffix to words ending in *ic*, add *ally* (basic/basically).
- *c* spells /k/ before *a, o, u*, and the consonants *l* or *r* (captain, company, current, climbed, crowd), and infrequently with other constructions, such as *ch* (chorus) and *cc* (occasion); *c* can spell /s/ before *e, i*, and *y* (groceries, accident, cyclone).
- using word origins, e.g., Latin *panis* = bread: com<u>pani</u>on (one who takes bread with you), com<u>pany</u> (a group taking bread together).

Spelling experiences should be integrated with opportunities for **language growth,** such as identifying and spelling **antonyms** (multiply/divide), **synonyms** (provide, furnish, equip, supply), **homophones** (continued practice with the most misused sets; expansion to less familiar homophones, e.g., current/currant, affect/effect, except/accept), **homographs** (contract), **idioms** (string along), **similes/metaphors** (as loud as thunder), **possessives** (boss's desk, doctors' orders), **regular** and **irregular plurals** (twenties, *o*-ending words, cactuses/cacti), **mispronounced words** (surprise, February), **contractions** (o'clock, they're, we're), **compound** words (breakfast), **multiple meanings** (charge), **analogies** (doctor : hospital :: president : office), **often-confused words** (breath/breathe), **usage** (lie/lay, further/farther, raise/rise, receive/accept), **abbreviations** (pound/lb.), **sorting words** (by meaning, phonetic analysis, structural attributes), **Greek** and **Latin roots** (vis/vid: television, video, visual, visit).

Students should explore **other word forms** of high-use writing words through the addition of all common **prefixes** and **suffixes**, and the **basic rules** that govern their use, particularly with **multisyllabic words**. Further, students should master **irregular verb forms**.

Explicit instruction in **visual skills** is essential, including the Word Preview—then students apply these skills in writing and proofreading.

Students need abundant **writing opportunities** to work toward the mastery of **Core Words** 1–1025, to grow them to many more words, and to maintain 100% accuracy in all everyday writing for **Priority Words** 1–130 (by the end of the school year).

Sitton Spelling and Word Skills®
3rd edition

Level 8

Skills and Concepts for Grade 8

An eighth grader's spelling experiences should include:

- **spelling by analogy** (occurring/rebelling/forgetting, canceling/modeling/motoring)
- **vowel spelling patterns** (review all previous patterns)
- **consonant spelling patterns and blends** (review all previous patterns)
- **irregular spellings** (rough, cantaloupe)
- **silent letters** (tongue, foreign)
- **spelling digraphs, diphthongs, and vowel-*r*** (review all previous patterns)
- **spelling soft-syllable endings** (ant/ent, ance/ence, able/ible, or/er/ar, al/el/le)
- **challenging letter groups** (ie/ei, ize/ise, ou)
- **challenging double-letter words** (recommend, address, immediately, employee, success)
- **foreign spellings** (Greek *ph* for /f/: telephone, and *ch* for /k/: character; French *ge* for /zh/: garage)

Further, students should learn **strategies** that enable them to anticipate the spelling and meaning of a word, such as:

- when adding the *ly* suffix to words that end in consonant-*y* (noisy, happy), change the *y* to *i* and add *ly* (noisily, happily).
- using word origins, e.g., Greek *tele* = far, *scope* = to see (telescope).

Spelling experiences should be integrated with opportunities for **language growth**, such as identifying and spelling **antonyms** (prevent/allow), **synonyms** (dangerous, hazardous), **homophones** (continued practice with the most misused sets; expansion to less familiar homophones, e.g., principle/principal, except/accept, council/counsel), **homographs** (progress, address, project, perfect), **possessives** (soldier's/soldiers'), **regular** and **irregular plurals** (oxen, activities, o-ending words), **mispronounced words** (environment), **contractions** (all accepted forms), **compound words** (newspaper, whenever), **multiple meanings** (address), **analogies** (forget : remember :: silent : noisy), **often-confused words** (angle/angel, lose/ loose, college/collage, message/massage), **idioms** (lose heart, string along), **similes/metaphors** (as proud as a peacock), **usage** (affect/effect), **abbreviations** (avenue/ave.), **sorting words** (by meaning, phonetic analysis, structural attributes, word origins), **Greek** and **Latin roots** (loc: locate, locality).

Students should explore **other word forms** of high-use writing words through the addition of all common **prefixes** and **suffixes**, and the **basic rules** that govern their use, particularly with **multisyllabic words**. Further, students should master **irregular verb forms**.

Explicit instruction in **visual skills** is essential, including the Word Preview—then students apply these skills in writing and proofreading.

Students need abundant **writing opportunities** to work toward the mastery of **Core Words** 1–1200, to grow them into many more words, and to maintain 100% accuracy in all everyday writing for **Priority Words** 1–130 (by the end of the school year).

INSIGHTS

Interesting Insights into English Spelling

Following are examples of discoveries students make as they explore spelling and language-related topics in the Sourcebook Series. Activities that foster discoveries help students become discriminating observers of words that enable them to grow into strategic, independent spellers.

Prefixes and Suffixes

- A prefix is a word part added to the beginning of a word or root to change its meaning.

  un + happy = unhappy

  When prefixes are added to words or roots, the spelling of the base word or root does not change.

  mis + spelling = misspelling, un + necessary = unnecessary

- A suffix is a word part added to the end of a word or root to change its use, or part of speech.

  teach + er = teacher
  Exceptions are the suffixes less and ful, which change meaning.

  When suffixes are added to words or roots, the spelling of the base word may change, but for most words or roots, the suffix is just added.

  help + s = helps

  However, when a <u>word or root ends in</u>—

- <u>silent e, drop the final e before adding a suffix that begins with a vowel</u>—
  a, e, i, o, u, y.

    fine + est = finest
  Exceptions include—
  - words such as mileage, acreage, and dyeing which retain the final e for pronunciation or to avoid confusion with another word.
  - words that end in ce or ge usually retain e if the suffix begins with a or o, such as noticeable and courageous.
  - words that end in ble, ple, or tle, drop the le before adding ly, such as possibly, simply, gently.
  - words in which the e is dropped before a suffix that begins with a consonant, such as ninth and judgment.

- <u>a stressed syllable that ends with one vowel and one consonant</u>, double the final consonant before adding a suffix that begins with a vowel—a, e, i, o, u, y.

    run + ing = running, begin + er = beginner
  Exceptions are words that end in w, x, or y, such as snowing, player, fixed.

- consonant-y, change y to i before adding a suffix, except those that begin with i.

    family + es = families

    rely + ing = relying

Exceptions exist, such as dryness.

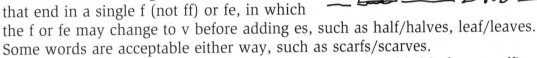

- s, sh, ch, x, or z, add es, not s.

    tosses, wishes, marches, mixes, fizzes

Exceptions include quiz, in which the z is doubled before adding es, and some words that end in a single f (not ff) or fe, in which the f or fe may change to v before adding es, such as half/halves, leaf/leaves. Some words are acceptable either way, such as scarfs/scarves.

- ic, the ly suffix becomes ally and the letter k is usually added before a suffix beginning with e, i, or y, such as basically and picnicking.

- o. If the word ends in vowel-o, s is added; for consonant-o, es is usually added.

    rodeo/rodeos, potato/potatoes

Exceptions include words of Italian origin (often musical terms) or Spanish origin, such as pianos and tacos. For some words, either s or es can be added, with one preferred.

Spelling Patterns

- Long e and long i sounds at the end of words are usually spelled y.

    copy, July

- The letter q is followed by u. Exceptions exist, such as Iraq.

- For words that end in /īz/, the spelling patterns are ize, ise, or yze. About nine out of ten /īz/ words are spelled ize, many are spelled ise, but very few use the yze pattern.

    organize, surprise, analyze

Some words with the ise pattern spell a different sound, such as promise.

- For words with the suffix pattern able/ible, able is about three times more common than ible. The base word provides little help to distinguish which suffix to use.

    audible/laudable, horrible/adorable, probable/possible/passable

- When /er/ follows w, the expected spelling pattern is or, such as in world.

- The ie/ei spelling pattern is erratic. Little help is offered to distinguish which to use.

    caffeine, brief

- One of the most reliable spellings is v spelling /v/, as in van. This occurs almost 100% of the time. **Of** course, you know the exception.

- For words with unstressed vowel-*r*, by far the most common pattern is er. This is followed by or, ar, and ure; and far less frequently by ur, our, eur, and re.

    dinner, equator, liar, pasture, murmur, glamour, amateur, massacre

- For words with the stressed vowel-*r*, the most common spelling patterns are er, ir, ur. The most frequent is er, but ir and ur are also prevalent.

    her, girl, turn

- The ance/ence patterns occur with about equal frequency. The ance spelling is used after the "hard" c (/k/) and after the "hard" g (/g/). The ence spelling is used after the "soft" c (/s/) and after the "soft" g (/j/). A y-ending verb requires the ance suffix in the noun form.

    significance/elegance, magnificence/intelligence, apply/appliance

- The ant/ent spelling patterns parallel the ance/ence patterns. The ant spelling is used after the "hard" c (/k/) and after the "hard" g (/g/). The ent spelling is used after the "soft" c (/s/) and after the "soft" g (/j/).

    vacant/elegant, innocent/detergent

- When /j/ follows a short vowel, it is usually spelled dge. When /j/ follows anything other than a short vowel, it is usually spelled ge.

    judge, large

- When /ch/ follows a short vowel, it is usually spelled tch. When /ch/ follows anything other than a short vowel, it is usually spelled ch.

    catch, lunch

- When /k/ follows a short vowel, it is usually spelled ck. When /k/ follows anything other than a short vowel, it is usually spelled k. A long vowel sound signals the ke pattern.

    back, mark, like

- The letter c spells /k/ almost three-fourths of the time. The next most common spelling is k, occurring 13% of the time. Other frequent patterns include ck, as in truck; ch, as in echo; qu, as in quiet. Infrequent patterns for /k/ include the French que, as in antique; kk, as in trekked; and cc, as in occasionally.

- At the end of a word, sede spells /sēd/ in one word—supersede, ceed in only three words—exceed, proceed, succeed, and cede in all other words—precede.

- The letter s spells /s/ almost three-fourths of the time. The next most common spelling for /s/ is c, occurring about 20% of the time. When c spells /s/, it is usually followed by e, i, or y. Other spellings for /s/ include ss and sc.

- The most frequent spelling pattern for /sh/ is ti, as in nation. This occurs about 53% of the time. The sh spells /sh/ about 26% of the time. Words with a French origin spell /sh/ with ch, as in chef. There are other less frequent /sh/ spellings, such as ce (ocean), ci (special), ss (pressure), si (mission), sci (conscious). Students discover that a single s spells /sh/ in only two words and their other word forms— sugar, sure.

- Spelling patterns for /ou/ are ou and ow (flour, flower). The ou pattern occurs about twice as often as ow. Yet, both ou and ow can spell other sounds. The ow is a frequent spelling pattern for /ō/ (snow).

- The ou vowel combination is the most deviant vowel pattern in English. It spells more sounds than any other vowel combination.

  tough, group, though, thought, fourth, bough, slough, hiccoughed

- Spelling patterns for /oi/ are oi and oy. At the beginning and in the middle of a word, both oi and oy can spell /oi/ (oil, point, oyster, voyage). At the end of a word, oy consistently spells /oi/ (boy, annoy). The oi pattern is more common.

- Long o occurs most often spelled o at the end of a syllable, as in hotel. This pattern accounts for about 73% of /ō/ words. The next most frequent spelling pattern is o-consonant-e, as in stone, occurring about 14% of the time. Other fairly frequent spelling patterns are oa, as in coast; ow, as in grown; and old, as in soldier. There are less frequently used patterns which include oe, as in toe; and ou, as in boulder.

- The most frequent /ī/ spelling patterns are i at the end of a syllable, as in library, and i-consonant-e, as in kite. Each pattern occurs in about 37% of /ī/ words, for a total of 74%. The next most frequent pattern is y at the end of a word, as in supply, occurring about 14% of the time. The igh pattern, as in high, and the ind pattern, as in behind, also regularly spell /ī/. Less frequent patterns for /ī/ include ie, as in tie.

- Long e occurs most often spelled e at the end of a syllable or word, such as in me, occurring in nearly 70% of /ē/ spellings. Other prevalent patterns are ee (need), y (study), and ea (meal). Less frequent options include ie (piece), i (ski), ei (receive), ey (monkey), and e-consonant-e (these).

- Most frequently, /ā/ is spelled a at the end of a syllable, as in table. This pattern occurs about 45% of the time. The next most frequent spelling pattern is a-consonant-e, as in cake, occurring about 35% of the time. Other frequent spelling patterns for /ā/ are ai, as in train, and ay, as in play. Less frequent options exist, such as ey in obey.

These research-based language and spelling insights are among the spelling conventions that students discover in Build Basic Concepts in the Sourcebook Series.

Spelling activities, such as those in Seeds for Sowing Skills, focus on providing students with many word experiences. Active word wall charts are useful toward this end. Following are ideas for primary, intermediate, and middle school/junior high teachers to make use of this strategy in their classroom.

Active Word Wall Charts for Developing Onsets and Rimes in a Primary Classroom

Opportunities to grow word banks through onsets and rimes (band, sand, hand) provide one example for using active word wall charts in the primary grades.

For example, label a chart __at. Ask students to find and write words to contribute to the chart. Some teachers do this as a class, but it can be done independently or in small groups. Students write their word contributions on sticky-note papers to attach to the chart, or on little slips of paper to place in a shoe box next to the chart. Later, the teacher writes the words on the chart. The list grows over time.

The purpose of this activity is not to teach/test students on the words collected, but to teach students how to make words.

These growing word banks can be used in multiple ways—have students:

- read the words
- spell the words as you touch each letter
- make rhymes with the words
- sort the words (e.g., doing words—verbs, and naming words—nouns).
- identify homophones, antonyms, or synonyms for the words
- add suffixes to the words

The opportunities for spelling and language development are immense!

CHECK OUT ANOTHER WAY TO BUILD SKILLS WITH — WORD WALL ACTIVITIES. See page 164

Active Word Wall Charts for Developing Phonics Understandings in Grades 3–5

Active word wall charts can engage students in more involved word finds that help students make generalizations about their language and how it is spelled. Just as in the primary grades, the purpose is to learn to make words, not to memorize spellings. For example, one activity could explore the options for spelling /k/. To commence, a chart is labeled with k and students begin their word hunts for words containing /k/ spelled with the letter k. These word collections can be group activities or occur independently between assignments, such as with the sticky-note method described in the primary example.

Soon students point out that /k/ can be spelled with c—only to discover that these are ca, co, cu, cl, and cr words. Then the collection of words naturally extends to charts for ch (character), qu for /kw/ (quick), cc (occasion), kk (trekked). Students also discover that ck can spell /k/ in the middle and at the end of words. Then the question is posed: What determines whether a /k/-ending word is spelled ck, k, or ke? In time, with the collection of more words, the students have the answer and can write the generalization—When /k/ follows a short vowel, it is usually spelled ck, and is usually spelled k or ke when it does not. A long vowel signals the ke pattern. Next, students are off and running finding exceptions! Will they discover the que endings on words with French origins or the English ic-ending words?

Active Word Wall Charts to Motivate Middle School/Junior High Students to Make Discoveries about Foreign Spellings

Middle school/junior high students have not outgrown active word wall charts. The concepts become more sophisticated, such as discovering spelling patterns of words with foreign origins. For example, words that reflect the Greek ph for /f/ pattern may be the subject of a word collection (e.g., physical, cellophane, apostrophe). A chart is labeled Words from the Greek—ph for /f/, and the word find begins.

The sticky-note method, as described in the primary example, works well for the collection of words, but sometimes students at this level can add words to the charts themselves. These students particularly enjoy playing in teams, but the word finds are immensely useful as sponge activities to productively "soak up" free time in between assignments. Teams can still be used because their independent contributions can be entered on the wall charts in their team color.

Students can be challenged to uncover other Greek spelling patterns with the letter p—pn (e.g., pneumonia), ps (e.g., pseudonym), and pt (e.g., ptomaine). Are there more examples of Greek spellings? Over time, students will uncover more Greek spellings, such as ch spelling /k/, rh spelling /r/, and x spelling /z/. As you work with synonyms, another Greek spelling will come to the fore—y spelling /i/—as in the word synonym, and the extensive word bank that reflects this pattern.

This concept can be expanded to French, Spanish, Italian, Latin, Native American, German, and Russian influences with active word wall charts. Each word bank results in generalizations about our language and its spellings that provide students the language skills they need for better thinking, speaking, writing, and reading. Watch your students' vocabularies grow as you employ active word wall charts.

HOW TO GIVE A CLOZE STORY WORD TEST

See www.sittonspelling.com, *Appleseed* e-Newsletter, January 2007, Sourcebook Teaching Tips, Cloze Story Word Test

PROCEDURES FOR FORMATIVE WORD TESTS

During the seminar, you were introduced to the formative tests, the Cloze Story Word Test and the Sentence Dictation Test, your two tests at the end of each spelling unit to assess all Core Words introduced so far in the program. These Core Words for each grade are listed alphabetically on a blackline master in each Sourcebook, and can be sent home at the beginning of the school year, if you wish.

The tests are diagnostic—they identify the current and all previously introduced Core Words in the program (all the way back to word number one, *the*) that each student has not mastered. The words students misspell or misuse on these tests are their unmastered words. These unmastered words become an individualized list of words for each student. These words are called their Spelling Words. So, the Cloze Story Word Tests and the Sentence Dictation Tests identify the Spelling Words, which are then targeted for study.

In addition to providing a personal study list of Spelling Words for each student, the tests evaluate spelling progress for a class and for individual students. For example, if on a given test sixteen students in your class miss the same word, you can compare this number with the results of subsequent tests in which the word is recycled. When these tests indicate that fewer students miss this word, measurable progress has been substantiated for this class with respect to that word. Further, each student's progress toward the mastery of the word can be observed.

Another function of the tests is to offer ongoing engagement with all current and previously introduced Core Words in the program. This repeated exposure contributes to their long-term mastery. The most often missed words, such as there/their/they're are recycled approximately one thousand times!

The Cloze Story Word Test is not as challenging as the Sentence Dictation Test. For students insufficiently challenged by the Cloze, use the Sentence Dictation—further, see Challenging the Capable Speller. For students overly challenged by the Cloze Story Word Test, see Students With Spelling Challenges.

Students do not know which words will be tested. To pinpoint the words a student has not yet mastered long term, test words cannot be practiced before the test. The tests must assess long-term mastery rather than short-term memory of words recently studied.

To test words using a Cloze Story Word Test, read the entire story aloud, including the test words, as students silently follow the story words with their eyes. Then read the story again, perhaps a sentence at a time, providing time for students to fill in the missing story words in the blanks. Finally, tell students to proofread their work by spelling each word silently or aloud as they touch each letter.

To test words using a Sentence Dictation Test, read the sentences aloud. Then read them again slowly to allow time for students to write the sentences. Use a brisk, but comfortable pace expecting students to listen carefully and write quickly. You may wish to read the sentences a third time. Finally, tell students to proofread.

If spelling references are not permitted, the tests function as a test of long-term spelling achievement. You may wish to allow students to use references—a valid test criterion, but not an assessment of long-term spelling achievement. Whether students use references or not, their work should be checked. Feedback on completed work is helpful to the learning process. You can check each test, or you may guide students through the correction procedure with students using a colored pencil to check their own or another student's test words.

You may ask students to work independently or together using spelling references to correct the spelling of their missed test words. You may wish to use a list of the Core Words introduced in the program through your grade level. This is on a blackline master in your Sourcebook (and is included as a personal reference in each Practice Book).

To grade a test, the number of words right or wrong on each student's test may be recorded to contribute to an evaluation of a student's overall spelling performance.

After students' tests are corrected, note if several students missed the same word(s). If so, follow up with a discussion, and then have students write the word(s) using the Word Study Strategy and/or have them write the words in sentences.

Further, students should record missed words in a Spelling Notebook. This is a pad of lined paper or a booklet made of a few sheets of students' writing paper with a construction paper cover. Students use it to record the words they missed on their Cloze Story Word Test or Sentence Dictation Test. These are a student's Spelling Words for at-school study. This makes a running record of errors. Routinely check students' Spelling Notebooks to make sure the words are spelled correctly and to identify words that recur. Then target students' study to recurring words.

Students should also record words missed on a Words to Learn sheet. This provides them with a personal study list of Spelling Words to take home. Each list is individualized to meet the spelling needs of each student. Students should study these words in preparation for subsequent Cloze Story Word Tests and Sentence Dictation Tests that automatically retest these words.

You, the student, or a parent may add words to the Words to Learn sheet in the More Words for Super Spellers section. These words should have writing relevance for the learner.

There is no need for you to keep a separate record of students' errors. The Spelling Notebook kept by each student keeps track of these words for at-school review, and their Words to Learn sheet lists the words for at-home study. The automatic recycling of Core Words is so extensive that by giving the Word Tests and the Sentence Dictation Tests regularly, students systematically revisit all words for ongoing practice to ensure their long-term mastery.

The use of the Cloze Story Word Test and Sentence Dictation Test differs greatly from testing with a customary Friday Test. Foremost, the objectives of the tests differ. The purpose of the Friday Test is to test the spelling words to determine students' grades. It culminates the unit and the study of a predetermined list of spelling words. The objective of the Cloze Story Word Test and Sentence Dictation Test is to make the teaching and learning of spelling more efficient by identifying the words students have not mastered. These become a student's Spelling Words—targeted for study. The Word Test and Sentence Dictation Test are diagnostic and initiate the study of individualized lists of Spelling Words for each learner that are automatically retested on subsequent tests. Further distinctions are noted on the next page.

The Cloze Story Word Test and Sentence Dictation Test, both formative assessments, are <u>different</u> from a Friday Test in—

1. Purpose

    Benefit: These tests gather information about words a student cannot spell to target practice for the long-term mastery of the words, while a Friday Test assesses short-term spelling retention and culminates the study of words.
    • A word-list test is not a formative assessment.

2. Pre/post study

    Benefit: When students prestudy the words just for the test, the test does not assess long-term mastery of words, but only short-term memory.

3. Assessment format

    Benefit: Assessment of words within the context of writing provides a more accurate assessment than words tested in isolation.

4. Options for testing

    Benefit: Multiple testing options within the program that include two tests of differing difficulty per unit increase flexibility to meet the needs of diverse learners and provide accurate feedback on progress, rather than one short-term memory test per unit.

5. Recycling of words

    Benefit: Conscientious study is enhanced when students know that words must be learned long-term rather than short-term; ongoing practice of words ensures their mastery. Repetition!

6. Learning outcome

    Benefit: Long-term learning of high-frequency words, rather than short-term learning of low-frequency words, enables students to write the words they need most often with ease and accuracy.

7. Time frame

    Benefit: An adjustable testing schedule provides teaching flexibility.

8. Length of list

    Benefit: A brief list of words individualized to a student's needs is superior to a lengthy list of predetermined words for a whole class.

THESE TESTS GATHER INFORMATION SO THAT INSTRUCTION AND PRACTICE CAN BE SPECIFICALLY TARGETED TO IMPROVE LEARNING.

Priority Words are the highest frequency words among the Core Words that form the basis for the program. Priority Words are your source for extending proof-reading practice to students' daily writing across the curriculum. Priority Words, sometimes referred to as "no excuses" words, are words that students are *always* accountable for in their everyday writing. The Priority Words designate a *minimum competency* for spelling. They do not designate all the words students would be spelling correctly in their everyday writing, nor alter the as-usual 100% accountability for every word on the final copy of a writing-as-a-process paper.

The highest-frequency word is *the*, so *the* is the first word to go on a Priority Word list in first grade. Then the next sequential words on a high-frequency word list are added to the Priority Word list. The number of Priority Words grows over time, from level to level, as students develop as spellers and writers. The list is cumulative—once a word is added, it stays.

At grade levels above grade one, the Priority Word expectation should begin with a realistic number of words to ensure success, but be perceived as easy to students. To determine this, look at the frequency-of-use list in this handbook or in the Priority Words Teaching Notes of a Sourcebook. Begin your Priority Word expectation with a sequential list beginning with *the* and including each sequential word up to the word that you anticipate students will likely miss in their writing.

Once the decision has been made regarding the number of words with which to start a Priority Word list, clearly state the expectations for spelling Priority Words. You may wish to have students write what they understood you to say. This ensures that they understand their new spelling-in-writing expectation and its consequences.

Students must be provided with an alphabetical list of Priority Words. How is this best achieved without having to remake the list each time a word is added? Many teachers use the Spell Check® cards that complement the Sourcebook Series. Use a colored marker to highlight students' current Priority Words on the cards. A regular highlighter makes a permanent mark on the coated paper. However, Priority Word lists can be teacher-made references, or for teachers with a Sourcebook, there is a Priority Words blackline master (and is included as a personal reference in each Practice Book).

Pace the addition of Priority Words. Add the words in order of frequency of use. The number of high-use words added at one time depends on the difficulty of the words and the ability of the students. At year's end, the correct spelling and use of all Priority Words recommended for the grade level should be routine with students. Remember, Priority Words are a minimum competency for spelling in everyday writing. The goal is not to have an extensive, challenging Priority Word list that students spell and use correctly in writing just sometimes, or even most of the time—but *all the time.*

In addition to Priority Words, students can be accountable for topical words, words students need for a particular assignment. Their spelling accuracy is expected on that one assignment. Then they are retired.

You may wish to add words to the Priority Word list permanently, such as your name, the name of your school, or the name of your city. These should be words students use often in writing. Write the words on a chart and post it in the classroom.

Priority Words suggested as a *minimum requirement* for mastery in writing by the *end of each grade level* are (for teachers with Sourcebooks, check for this information in your Priority Words Teaching Notes)—

- level 1: high-frequency words 1–15 (*Too* of the *to/two/too* homophones can be omitted until second grade.)
- level 2: high-frequency words 1–35 (Add *too* to the *to/two/too* homophones.)
- level 3: high-frequency words 1–55 (The *there/their/they're* and *your/you're* homophones can be omitted.)
- level 4: high-frequency words 1–75 (Add *there/their/they're* and *your/you're*. You can omit *there's/theirs*.)
- level 5: high-frequency words 1–100 (Add *there's/theirs*.)
- levels 6–8: high-frequency words 1–130

Although words are usually added to the Priority Word list in order of frequency of use in writing, if you prefer to add a word sooner or later than its frequency designates, you may do so.

Most of the students in a classroom have the same Priority Word expectation. Yet, you may wish to have a lower expectation (fewer words) for less able students and a higher expectation (more words) for the most capable students. This deserves a word of caution. Students who cannot read English should not be in a formal spelling program, nor have a Priority Word list (see Students With Spelling Challenges). To challenge able students, a lengthy Priority Word list is not as an effective differentiating strategy as challenging them through other aspects of the program (see Challenging the Capable Speller).

You can determine the level of responsibility required for homophones. Often, when one homophone is added, the responsibility for its partner(s) is also added. Yet, let your common sense guide you. For example, first grade students can learn to be responsible for the homophones *to* and *two*. Then *too* can be added in second grade. Further, second graders can be responsible for *four* when word number 11, *for*, is added, but not *fore*. The homophone set *there/their/they're/there's/theirs* is the most difficult set of words to add to the list, but once *there*, number 37, is added, *their* and *they're* should also be included. Later, *there's* and *theirs* can be added.

To help students differentiate homophones, use context sentences. Context sentences for high-use homophones are provided on the back of the 3–8 Spell Check® card. Context sentences on classroom posters are also helpful.

Other levels of Priority Word responsibility are yours to decide, for example, the use of *a* for *an*. If students have letter reversals, should this be considered an error? It depends on the student and your perception of his/her current capacity to write without reversals. Use your best judgment on individual issues, such as these.

Specific time to proofread should accompany each written task. Students can proofread independently or with their classmates. Keep students focused during the proofreading sessions by walking about the classroom giving general proofreading pointers. Perhaps, set a timer to indicate time solely for proofreading. Be persistent, yet positive. Ongoing, enthusiastic emphasis on Priority Words helps students make these words a priority *before* their papers are handed in—not afterward, making more work for you. The goal is to guide students toward their own proofreading success. Celebrate this success overtly! No one ever tires of hearing they're successful.

Students' ability to spell and use their Priority Words correctly in their everyday writing should be evaluated. Assessment is made by looking at students' writing. About once a week (less often in middle school/junior high English classes), select a piece of writing from each student. Students should not be told how often a sample will be selected or which piece of writing will be reviewed. They simply know that papers are being selected, unannounced, for evaluation of spelling in writing. Bracket a section of the writing to evaluate—perhaps one sentence in grade one, two to three sentences in grades two and three, and a short paragraph in the upper grades. This is the sample from which you make your assessment.

Although evaluating all of every student's writing would be more thorough, it is unnecessary. Spelling evaluation should replicate reading evaluation. Judgments are made on students' reading abilities based on samples of oral reading. Hearing the whole book would be more thorough, but it is unnecessary. Likewise, you can make a sound judgment of students' spelling abilities by evaluating only a section of their writing. Time is limited.

When Priority Words are made a priority, the result is no Priority Word errors. This is as it should be, inasmuch as the Priority Word requirement represents the *minimum expectation* for spelling in writing. Yet, if a student does not meet this requirement on a writing sample selected for evaluation, then the error should be noted. For example, place a dot in the margin next to the line of writing in which the error appears. The student corrects the error and returns the paper to you. Keep these papers (or a copy) in an assessment file folder for each student. This ongoing data documents each student's ability to meet the Priority Word requirement.

Writing samples do not need to be graded. Students either meet the minimum requirement for spelling in everyday writing, or they do not. This information should contribute to the total spelling evaluation for each student.

Occasionally, you may wish to judge a piece of students' everyday writing without the use of their Spell Check® reference. This writing is called a no-reference write. Further, Priority Words are among the bank of words tested in the Cloze Story Word Tests and Sentence Dictation Tests, so routine use of the tests in the program automatically assesses Priority Words without the use of references.

Parents can be allies as you develop proofreading skills. Written assignments from across the curriculum can be graded for the subject in which they were written, then sent home for parent-child proofreading. Mark the paper with a "Proofread with Me" signal that indicates to parents that this was not checked by you for spelling so that they could work with their child toward this end. Instruct parents not to proofread the paper for their child, but to assist them. Suggest that parents place a dot in the margin next to a line that has an error to help their child locate, then fix, the mistake.

The goal is for students to spell and proofread their Priority Words effortlessly in all their writing. This has benefits. Even for adults, the words most frequently misspelled and misused are within the 100 highest-frequency writing words. Every teacher's dilemma is how to teach students to eliminate these careless errors from their writing. The ongoing attention to Priority Words not only achieves this objective, but helps students learn to proofread *for all words*.

Once these high-use words are committed to memory, writing fluidity is significantly increased. Students no longer struggle with the spelling and use of the most basic words. Now they can mature as writers. Further, scores on standardized spelling tests and performance-based measurements increase when students learn the skills these tests assess—proofreading. The Priority Word focus of this program provides students with conscientious attention to proofreading—instruction, daily practice, evaluation, and feedback on their performance.

Perhaps the greatest benefit is that students learn they can spell words correctly, making each writing experience an easier and more positive one. Success is an ongoing motivator to make every child a speller!

Teach visual skills.
>Word Preview (see suggestions, this handbook)
>Word Study Strategy (see suggestions, this handbook)
>Visual skill-building activities (see suggestions, this handbook)
>Activities labeled visual skill building (Sourcebook Series)

Model proofreading.
>Demonstrate strategies, such as—
>>1. Read writing aloud and touch each word.
>>2. Look for specifics one at a time—Priority Words, topical words, homophones, grammar (a/an), plurals.
>>3. Proofread from right to left (upper grades only).
>>4. Circle questionable words. Then check spellings using a reference.
>>5. Once 1–4 have been completed, carefully reread the writing.

Proofread with a partner.
>Demonstrate cooperative efforts to proofread sections of writing together.

Monitor proofreading.
>Circulate among students as they proofread to keep them on task. The better this task is done, the less correcting there is for both teachers and students later.

Credit proofreading.
>No one tires of compliments for a job well done. Always try to find some aspect of the proofreading process to credit each student. Celebrate success.

Support students for whom proofreading is a challenge.
>Always set realistic proofreading expectations for Priority Words for lower performing students, but never relax the 100% standard. Identify sections of writing to proofread one at a time, rather than to have a student proofread an entire paper.

Involve parents.
>Send papers home not marked at school for Priority Words. Ask parents to support proofreading by routinely assisting their child to proofread these papers. Forewarn parents not to be the "editor," but to place a dot in the margin next to a line of writing in which there is an error. The child should identify the error. Then the parent and the child can verify the spelling and the child can make the correction.

Remember—all spelling performance tests are proofreading/editing tests!

ASSESSING
SPELLING
PROGRESS

LET'S EVALUATE

This is your source for an overview of the extensive formal and informal options available to assess students' spelling progress. You can develop an assessment model that meets your evaluative needs from among several formative testing options discussed in the seminar.

The purpose for each evaluation option is to maximize teaching and learning efficiency by providing information to target study and instruction to students' needs. In addition, the evaluations communicate to students that the reason they learn to spell is for writing, not for a single test. Further, the evaluations offer teachers the opportunity to validate spelling growth for a school, a class, and for individual students. These objectives differ significantly from that of a customary spelling program.

In a customary program, the evaluation, usually limited to a weekly Friday spelling test, culminates a spelling unit. Its primary purpose is to provide a means of grading students, albeit on their short-term memory capacity. This process serves to communicate to students that the reason they learn to spell is for the test. They study the words just prior to the test for scoring well on the test.

This not only misleads students, but results in short-term learning that handicaps students for spelling well in writing—a process that requires long-term mastery of words. Therefore, assessment must change. To reverse the short-term learning mind-set that obstructs attaining spelling success in writing, evaluation that delivers long-term learning must replace a cause of the problem—the Friday Test. This program offers that opportunity through tests that provide ongoing data to improve instruction and practice.

Develop your assessment model as a grade-level group to ensure uniformity. Here are options, all formative assessments, each a component of the Sourcebook Series:

1. Assess students' ability to meet the minimum requirement for spelling in everyday writing—**Priority Words**—as well as any topical words identified for accuracy for a particular assignment.

2. Assess students' mastery toward spelling the high-frequency Core Words tested on the **Cloze Story Word Tests** and the **Sentence Dictation Tests**. They are administered as a group test, yet the results are differentiated to each student's spelling needs. The words students miss become their Spelling Words. All words are recycled continuously so that retesting students' words occurs automatically through subsequent tests. The bank of words from which these tests assess spelling are *all words* beginning with the first word on a word-frequency list up to the current Core Word for the grade level. Spelling references are not allowed during the administration of these tests.

3. Assess students' ability to apply essential spelling and language-related skills on a **Skill Test**. Usually a customary program assesses only words, yet the ability to generalize spelling principles ensures that students can apply their knowledge for learning to spell hundreds of words and to proofread for them in writing.

4. Assess students' performance on selected skill-building exercises from the menu of suggested **Sourcebook activities.** These may include practice from the Exercise Express (Build Spelling and Language Skills), Seeds for Sowing Skills (Build Basic Concepts), Test Ready (Build Assessment Readines), or any other assigned Sourcebook activity. Students' performance provides ongoing formal or informal diagnostic information not only for student grading, but data for the teacher to make informed activity selections in subsequent units.

5. Assess students' performance on **Practice Book activities**. These optional activities provide follow-up to specific Sourcebook lessons or supplement the lessons by introducing extension word work.

6. Assess students' ability to perform on **proofreading tests**—the Proof It activity that occurs in every Sourcebook unit (grades 5–8) and in every Practice Book unit (grades 1–6). All use formats that are facsimiles of the most often-used standardized tests and achievement tests. All test spelling as well as other editing elements.

Further, your assessment model may also include students' ability to produce an error-free final paper, the last stage in any writing process. It may take into account how well students spell in everyday writing when, on occasion, you do not allow the use of references. Some teachers may wish to figure in students' performance on the Sourcebook Achievement Tests (three tests spaced throughout the school year on black-line masters with cloze/writing format choices).

Your assessment model should reflect a unified decision from teachers at a given grade level and specify the relative weight or percent of the total grade on the assessments you choose to use. By the way, this can change. Revisit and, if necessary, revise your assessment model at the start of any new grading period.

Once constructed, your evaluation procedures should be communicated to students and parents. Explain the grading system and tell them what they can do to increase achievement. Constructive, ongoing evaluation positively impacts spelling growth to make every child a speller!

Here is an example of a Spelling Progress Report developed by teachers dissatisfied with the format on their current report card. Teachers, parents, and students all say that it better addresses real spelling issues.

Name_____

SPELLING PROGRESS REPORT

Marking Code:
3 (exceeds expectations)
2 (meets expectations)
1 (falls below expectations)

Grading Quarters	1st	2nd	3rd	4th
Uses correct spelling in everyday writing	___	___	___	___
Completes spelling skill-building activities	___	___	___	___
Shows improvement on spelling tests	___	___	___	___

Parent Signature _____
_____
_____
_____

Increasing Spelling Test Scores

Educators want to increase students' ability to spell well—mainly because they care about their students' well-being. In the workplace, few learning deficiencies are so visibly debilitating as poor spelling. Further, there is another reason teachers are concerned about their students' spelling and word-skill proficiency. Scores for these tests may even be posted on the Internet by district, school, and classroom. How can educators rise to the challenge to teach spelling and related skills so that concrete growth can be ensured?

First, it's important to note how these tests assess spelling. All use a proofreading/editing format. Therefore, proofreading and editing skills must be taught, practiced, and assessed. Further, the tests often use unfamiliar words so that the upper limits of student performance can be evaluated. So, students need exposure to many words, as well as a foundation in basic skills and concepts to allow them to generalize about the spelling of words with which they have no experience.

Students engaged in the methodology of the Sourcebook Series show increases in spelling test scores—the district/state/standardized achievement and/or performance tests. Further, educators report that students' scores on related language and word skills improve, such as vocabulary development. Following are factors that contribute to students' score increases—

- Students receive *extensive instruction and practice in visual skill building*. These skills are essential for successful proofreading.

- Students are held *accountable for proofreading* their Priority Words in their everyday writing and are evaluated on their ability to meet a stated expectation.

- Teachers in the program provide students with *strategies for proofreading*—reminding students to proofread does not constitute instruction.

- Students are *tested on proofreading* in every unit of the Sourcebook on the Proofreading Test, grades 5–8, and in every unit's Proof It test in the student Practice Books, grades 1–6. These tests use the same format as actual tests to make students test-wise.

- Students learn essential *skills and concepts to make generalizations* about hundreds of words and their spellings. They become discriminating observers of words to allow them to strategize the spellings of unknown words.

- Each student's Spelling Words are identified from among all words previously introduced in the program, targeted for study, and then *recycled to ensure their long-term mastery*.

- *Spelling skills are tested* to ensure a proper spelling foundation.

- *Achievement Tests* gather information to assess students' progress over time.

This is your source for suggestions to meet the needs of students challenged by spelling. These are students who learn to spell more slowly, students for whom English is not their native language, and transfer students who lack spelling skills.

Spelling ability is not related to intelligence—all students can learn to spell. Some students have a greater propensity for spelling than others, but this is true of any ability. An obstacle that must be overcome with these learners is that some have learned they "can't spell." This message is delivered by frequent Friday Test failures in a program that equates spelling proficiency with memorization of words for a test. This "disability" may be reinforced by classmates, parents, and a low spelling grade on a report card. Whether students think they can spell, or whether they think they cannot spell—they're right.

Foremost in this methodology is to provide multiple options to productively involve all students in spelling and language-related learning at their level. When challenged students can note their own personal progress, the message they receive is, "I can." Their success is a powerful motivator with a dividend that *increases* effort on their part—yet *decreases* the time and effort you must exert toward their instruction.

WHAT IT TAKES TO LEARN TO SPELL —

There are prerequisites to spelling success. The first is a facility with English. Language learning is developmental. Stated simplistically, speaking the language is the first step; reading is the next step. Spelling can commence when students have mastered a basic reading vocabulary, learned the names of the letters and can write each letter, and understand that these letters make words. Until these conditions are satisfied, attempting to teach a learner to spell is inappropriate.

Basic contributors to spelling success are visual skills, the ability to remember what words look like, application of phonics generalizations to spell words, and use of analogous thinking to make words through spelling word patterns and other word forms. Students need to be taught strategies to spell and proofread words. They need many opportunities to work with words to learn about such things as homophones, apostrophes, and the most useful spelling rules—particularly for plurals and suffixes. Research supports a correlation between spelling success and time spent practicing these skills.

These are experiences that students challenged by spelling need, indeed need more of than students for whom spelling is easy. Yet, because of the wide range of activity and testing options in this program, only minor modifications need to be made to accommodate students with spelling challenges. These few adaptations are easily made.

Program Adaptations for Students with Spelling Challenges

 When giving the Word Preview, prepare an activity sheet for which you use a highlighter to write in the Core Words to be written in the write column. Instead of writing the words, these students trace the words. Then they rewrite the words in the rewrite column using the traced words as a model. This includes them in the class activity and provides an opportunity to trace and learn to read the words.

 Modifications can be made to the Word Preview for students who find it difficult to copy from the chalkboard. One modification is to pair these students with able learners. As these capable students write the words in the rewrite column of their paper, they say the name of each letter just audibly enough for their partner to hear. This provides an auditory cue that makes the activity far easier. Another modification uses cards on which Core Words for the Word Preview have been written. When the class is copying the word from the chalkboard, the challenged students copy the word from the word card. Over time, the Word Preview modifications can be phased out.

 These students benefit from abundant language experiences. The activities in this program are rich in language-integrated learnings that contribute extensively toward this end. For example, the Exercise Express and Seeds for Sowing Skills activities demonstrated in the seminar and described in this handbook range in difficulty, and are recycled extensively. Therefore, skills and activities can be selected that specifically meet students' needs. Some direction or monitoring will be necessary for students who cannot work independently in order for them to benefit from these activities. You, an aide, or another student can provide assistance. In addition, participating in a cooperative group or observing the class discussion of these activities is productive for students challenged by spelling.

 A wide body of evidence clearly shows that experiences with literature are basic to the development of measurable growth in students' language skills. This suggests the inclusion of skill-building activities relating to literature. Engage the students' parents, an older student, or an aide to read and reread the books to or with these learners. Follow-up with writing activities—shared ones between the mentor and the student.

 Students challenged by spelling struggle with writing. To develop their writing and spelling skills, they benefit from both modeled writing (where you are responsible for the content and the actual writing) and guided writing (where you and the students construct the content, but you do the writing with spelling suggestions from students). When students write independently, accept all invented spellings in their writing until they have developed sufficient proficiency to participate in the Priority Word routine. Begin with only one or two Priority Words, even though other students are responsible for more.

Writing-as-a-process papers require 100% spelling accuracy on the final copy, a standard that is difficult for these students. You may wish to relax the expectation of a 100% error-free standard to one section of a writing piece. However, this would not result in a paper appropriate for "publishing." Another option is to divide the task into doable portions until the entire paper is error-free. Work with a small section of a paper at a time in brief work sessions.

 Challenged students can participate in the Cloze Story Word Test, although modifications may be needed. For example, for English-language learners who cannot read English, use a highlighter to write all the test words in the blanks. Instead of writing the words, they trace the words as the test is given. This serves to include them in the class activity and provides an opportunity to trace and learn to read the words. This modification can be adapted to students' abilities. Use a highlighter to write in selected words on their copy of the test. They trace these words and spell the others. The words they are asked to spell are their test words. Choose the highest-frequency words for test words, because they are more useful for writers than words with lower frequencies that occur less often in writing. Words misspelled on the Word Test, as with the other students, become students' spelling words for study.

 If students need guidance with the Skill Test, provide help with the directions and expectations. If the test is still too challenging, elicit oral answers from them while other students are taking the test independently.

 The Sentence Dictation Test is more challenging than the Cloze Story Word Test. If students have difficulty with the Cloze Story Word Test, do not give them the Sentence Dictation Test as an assessment of spelling achievement. However, the additional practice the Sentence Dictation Test provides is beneficial. You may wish to provide a reference for the sentences after the students have written them. This offers proofreading practice and practice using a reference. The more students are exposed to the words they need to learn, the more expedient the process of mastering them becomes.

A SPECIAL NOTE FOR SPECIAL NEEDS TEACHERS

For Special Needs educators, instruction can be provided in the level of the program that best approximates students' reading level (e.g., Level 2 for students reading at second grade). Because each Sourcebook includes multiple activities in each unit that are above and below grade level, you can accommodate a range of abilities in the same Sourcebook for your instruction. Extra structure and additional reinforcement can be provided with the Practice Books, Levels 1–6 (see page 161).

THE CAPABLE SPELLER

This is your source for ideas to challenge the most capable spellers—students whose spelling abilities surpass the basic program expectations at their grade level. These students:

- complete skill-building activities successfully,
- spell and use all of the required Priority Words correctly in their everyday writing all of the time, not most of the time,
- spell and use most words beyond the Priority Word expectation correctly in their everyday writing,
- score 100% on the Cloze Story Word Tests (without prestudying words),
- apply skills tested on the Skill Tests, and
- use a reference to spell topical words correctly.

Following are suggestions to challenge students—

 Select the most challenging skill-building activities for these students. They benefit from activities that focus on sorting words, multiple meanings, making hypotheses, idiomatic usage, word origins, and making extended word collections from which to make spelling generalizations.

 Direct one part of an activity to the class. Then have the most able students follow up with another part of the activity independently. On occasion, ask them to present their work to the class so that all students can benefit from the activity—perhaps in both written and oral form.

 All students should take the Cloze Story Word Test. It is unusual for students to score 100% on this test consistently—remember, students never prestudy the words. For more challenge use the Sentence Dictation Test. It assesses more words; requires more listening and writing; and evaluates mechanics, including capitalization and punctuation. Further, Extra Words (words beyond the Core Words) in Sentence Dictation Tests serve to challenge students. To expedite administering the Sentence Dictation Test to a few students, ask a student to dictate the sentences. Then have students exchange papers and correct the tests using a copy of the Core Words for a spelling reference.

 More Words For Super Spellers, a section on the Words to Learn study list, can challenge the able learner. You, the student, or a parent may add words with writing relevance to this list for at-home study.

 An at-school challenge list can be compiled to replicate and/or complement the at-home challenge list. Have students record challenge words in their Spelling Notebook. Then students can assess each other on these words periodically.

Capable students can be challenged with an extended Priority Word list and topical word list.

 Use the complementary materials for Levels 1–3 for exciting extensions—Word Skills in Rhythm and Rhyme and the Core Word Activity Cards (see page 164).

 Ask able students to assist other students as they proofread and revise their papers.

 For a motivational writing project, these students could work independently, with a teacher assistant, or with an older student to:
- publish a monthly news bulletin to parents
- write book reviews for a class "Recommended Reading" journal
- develop a buyer's guide for a product students often purchase
- make a joke or riddle book
- create a weekly comic strip
- write the lyrics to students' favorite songs
- create books for the school or classroom library
- take notes at class meetings and rewrite the minutes for the class record
- write a play and present it to the class
- make school posters on a timely topic, such as safety
- create spelling crossword or word-search puzzles for their classmates
- assemble a cookbook for kids' snacks
- write sequels to favorite fairy tales, fables, or stories
- create a telephone directory for students
- write the rules to favorite games
- review movies or new TV shows
- compile information on word lore
- create a class "nickel-ads"
- develop a school or community Who's Who? with mini-biographies
- research and write an extension to a science or social studies lesson
- create an advice column
- make bookmarks, each with a famous saying
- keep an ongoing list of lost-and-found articles for school dissemination
- create a monthly class or school calendar
- write announcements and follow-up reviews of current sporting events
- compile word collections on a particular topic, such as things you would find on a dairy farm

 Have students create their own Exercise Express activities, crossword puzzles, and other games to challenge each other.

 Write! Don't forget the writing follow-ups after the Cloze Story Word Tests and Sentence Dictation Tests.

Use the "apple" extension ideas on every page of the optional student Practice Books, Levels 1–6 (see page 161).

This is your source to cultivate parent support.

Tell Parents About Your Program Before You Begin

As you implement the program, inform parents why a change was made in spelling and how the new program will help to achieve your goal. You may wish to do this in a meeting for parents. Explain how the Sourcebook Series is different from a customary program, why it's different, and how they can participate to help their child succeed.

- Be sure parents receive a copy of the Introducing Spelling Blackline Master (in Sourcebooks).
- Have Sourcebooks available for parents to peruse.
- Use the Tutor Me CD-ROM Parent Introduction (see page 162) or the free Series Overview (see page 160).
- Explain your grading system.
- Consider demonstrating an activity from the Build Skills and Word Experiences section of a unit and/or a Cloze Story Word Test.
- Garner more ideas from veteran Sourcebook teachers (see page 84).

Keep Parents Informed and Involved Throughout the Year

Continue to keep parents informed, and provide opportunities for them to be involved. Besides reading the Parents as Partners Teaching Notes in your Sourcebook, consider these options—

 Use these blackline masters in the Sourcebooks:
- Take-Home Tasks (skill-building activities for every unit)
- Core and/or Priority Word Lists (reference lists)
- Exercise Express (six activities in every unit on generic blackline masters)
- Word Preview (for visual skills)
- Personal Posters (masters that parallel classroom teaching posters)
- Word Study Strategy (for independent study)
- Bonus Masters (extra blackline masters in Level 1)
- Literature Lists (for literature tie-in activities)

 Some teachers also send home tests once they have been completed for each unit—
- Cloze Story Word Tests (on blackline masters)
- Skill Tests (on blackline masters)

- Proofreading Tests (on blackline masters)
- Sentence Dictation Tests

◑ Spelling Words can be sent home for each unit on:
- Words to Learn Blackline Master (lists the Spelling Words), along with
- Ideas for Word Study Blackline Master (suggestions for learning words "forever") (Copy these two masters back-to-back.)

◑ Papers for proofreading that were purposely not marked for Priority Words can be sent home with:
- Ideas for Proofreading Blackline Master (suggestions for refining proofreading skills)

◑ Provide ongoing homework activities from the Sourcebook's menus of activity ideas—such as the collection of word banks; writing follow-ups from Word Tests, Sentence Dictation Tests, and Proofreading Tests; Did You Know? and Word Mysteries & Histories features; Build Skillful Writers exercises; Cloze Story Word Test extension activities; and the "apple" extension ideas on every page of the optional student Practice Books, Levels 1–6 (see page 161).

◑ Provide an invitation for parents to help at school—such as assisting students as they proofread, checking tests, checking the spelling of words on the Words to Learn sheets or in the Spelling Notebooks, and guiding students with the Word Study Strategy.

There are ample opportunities for parent-child spelling partnerships. Your commitment to ongoing opportunities for parents to participate in their child's education is essential whether or not parents exercise interest. Few parents are not interested, but some parents have more time and facility for partaking in these activities.

Parents who are not native English speakers may be unable to offer their child assistance. For these families, communicate the power of an enthusiastic attitude toward school. The skills their child is learning can help all learners, making your school program one that fosters adult literacy.

For families who do not support their child, the burden falls on you. This means more must take place in the classroom. Accommodate this within a reasonable time frame. What is not accomplished at one grade is taken on in the next. This program recycles skills and words so that each grade overlaps to reconcile different achievement levels to make every child a speller.

Provide Parents with Options for Getting Their Questions About Spelling Answered

- Visit the web site—www.epsbooks.com/sittonspelling
- Invite parents to visit their child's classroom to see the program in action.
- Provide an opportunity for parents to revisit the Tutor Me Parent Introduction CD-ROM (see page 162).

Veteran Teachers Offer Suggestions to Ensure Parent Support

GETTING STARTED MEANS GETTING _parents_ STARTED ON A NEW BACK-TO-BASICS SPELLING PROGRAM!

What could be more basic?
   ...spelling expectations in writing...skills...
   spelling tests without getting the answers ahead of time...

Each year, more teachers at our school use the Sourcebooks. However, because not all teachers use the program, I explain it to parents at Back-to-School night. Last year, I had parents of my last year's students come in and tell about the program and the progress their child made. It was fantastic! But, this year our testing interfered with Back-to-School night and it wasn't scheduled until just before the holidays. That was too late! So, I had parents write about their experiences with their child's spelling, and tell why they thought it was better than the old program. I made copies (with permission), and sent them home. "Parents telling parents" about the Sourcebooks is a way that I highly recommend starting.

Martha Samson
Third Grade Teacher

I teach a 4–5 multiage class. I felt comfortable explaining to my students how the new program was different, and my students accepted my explanation with enthusiasm. They knew that in their old program they just studied the words for the test! Yet, I wasn't as confident about explaining the program to the parents of my students. What to do? A colleague of mine gave me this idea, and it worked!

I asked my students to select a medium to highlight the difference between our old spelling and our new spelling. For this project, I suggested a poster, a poem, a skit, a story—whatever a student wanted to do to make this point. Students shared their projects with classmates. Then they took their project home with the Introducing Spelling blackline master. Their job was to explain to those at home how our new spelling would be different. My students did a great job, because parents were excited, pleased, and eager to become more familiar with "forever spelling."

Janet Beech
Fourth–Fifth Multiage Teacher

The parents in our district always seemed to want long lists of words. We were afraid that the words on the Words to Learn sheet wouldn't be enough, yet we didn't want to compromise the Sourcebook philosophy by adding extra words to make it look "hard" for parents. This is what we did. We used an idea in the Parents as Partners section of our Sourcebooks and duplicated the Core Words blackline master on heavy stock to send home. We told parents that these words, or forms of these words, would be tested unannounced throughout the year. If their child missed a word or two, the word(s) would be sent home on a Words to Learn sheet—now they *didn't expect long lists*. To help their child at home, they could do the same thing, with the goal of making sure that their child could spell these words *anytime*. They liked it, and they worked on the words with their child, and *everyone won*, including the kids!

Ben Fidymann
Sixth Grade Lead Teacher

To prove that we needed to make big changes in spelling, we went to the high school in our unit and asked the English teachers to help us. We wanted papers that were written and supposedly proofread by capable students who usually got A's in spelling in the elementary schools. We wanted to prove that even if kids could spell on spelling tests at the lower grades, it was no proof that they'd apply the skills in high school.

It was really something! We had more papers than we could ever use—all with careless misspellings. We removed students' names, made transparencies, and showed the examples to parents at the opening of a Spelling Meeting we held at school on two afternoons and one evening. Parents could attend the one they wanted. At the meeting we explained the new program briefly, gave them a copy of the Introducing Spelling blackline master, and provided them an on-loan copy of the Overview Video about the Sourcebooks. No problems! And now we have kids that can spell!

Olivia Alexander
Unit Leader/Elementary Pod

We decided to start our Sourcebook program in our district after conferences. At each conference, we asked parents if they'd support the idea of expecting their child to spell correctly in their writing, not just on tests. Not one parent disagreed! We explained the Priority Words, and gave them a copy of the Priority Words blackline master. Then we explained the skill activities in a nutshell—mainly that the program focused on skills, as in reading, and that they'd get skill activities to do with their child on Take-Home Tasks. Then we told them that we'd be testing all grade-level and previous grade-level words systematically to be sure their child knew them, and we gave them a copy of the Core Words blackline master—the words that would be tested.

Then we told them about the three things we'd grade—how well students did on their Priority Words, their Take-Home Tasks (which we required be returned to school), and their Core Word tests. Parents were immensely supportive, and still are!

Heidi Elmhurst-Quismo
Fourth Grade Teacher

WORD STUDY

The Word Study Strategy is your source for teaching your students the five research-based steps to learn to spell a word. The dominant modality is visual. For students to use this strategy effectively, the steps need to be modeled, then reviewed over time.

1. Read the word.
2. Spell the word—touch each letter and say its name.
3. Cover the word.
4. Print the word.
5. Proofread the word—touch each letter and say its name.

For step one, write a word on the chalkboard. Read the word aloud. Tell students that when they use the strategy they may read the word aloud or silently. Then model how a learner can think about the word. Ask questions, such as—

- Does this word look like another word I know?
- Does this word sound like another word I know?
- Is this word a homophone?
- Where have I seen this word before?

In step two, spell the word aloud. Touch each letter with the chalk as its name is said. Students may spell the word aloud or silently as they use the procedure. Then direct students' attention to further analyze the word by asking questions, such as—

- How many letters are in this word?
- Are there double letters?
- Is the word spelled the way it sounds?
- Are there silent letters?
- Do I see a spelling pattern in this word?
- Do I see a base word in this word?
- Is there an apostrophe in this word?
- Is this word spelled with a capital letter?
- How many tall letters do I see?
- How many tail letters do I see?
- Is there a jingle that helps to spell the word?
- Is there anything special about this word to help remember its spelling?

Then demonstrate step three. Cover the word with your hand or a sheet of paper.

Next, model step four. Demonstrate printing the word on the chalkboard. Tell students that you are picturing each letter in your mind as you print the word.

Last, demonstrate how to proofread the word. Uncover the original word. Tell students that to proofread the word, each letter is matched with the same letter in the original word. Show students how to touch each letter of the word and say its name as you match the letters. Point out how your eyes go back and forth from the original word to the word written for practice as the letters are matched.

Then tell students it's their turn to practice the study steps. You may wish to use the Word Study Strategy Blackline Master for practice, however, if the steps are posted in the classroom, regular writing paper is sufficient.

Multiage instructional units productively use this methodology because of its flexibility. Students who vary widely in spelling and language-related abilities can be accommodated with only minor modifications.

Multiage students can be instructed in the same unit of the same level of the series, but their learning programs nonetheless reflect extensive diversity. To begin, select a teaching level in which the lowest performers are challenged. Then make modifications to meet all learners' needs.

For example, the most sophisticated exercises in the Seeds for Sowing Skills can be selected for students who need a challenge, while the less difficult exercises can be reserved for students who are not yet ready for the most demanding tasks. Each concept is supported by activity options that range widely in difficulty. Because skills are systematically recycled, students who are initially challenged by a task grow with each exposure. This is true for each of the unit sections.

Students challenged by the level of difficulty of an activity require more direction. This can be provided by you, but able learners can often mentor students who need assistance—one of the benefits of multiage learning. This support allows you to divide your instructional time more equitably among all learners in the classroom.

For testing, again the program flexibility allows for diversity. For example, the Cloze Story Word Test can be altered significantly to make it less demanding, while the Sentence Dictation Test can be reserved for students who would benefit from additional practice or more challenge.

As you implement the Priority Words, diversity can exist in the expectation for spelling accuracy, but not the standard set for spelling the words. All students should be afforded a Priority Word list for which 100% accuracy is the standard. It is generally recommended that Priority Word expectations be confined to no more than three different lists within the same classroom to maintain ease in management.

Specific ideas for modification can be gathered from Challenging the Capable Speller and Students With Spelling Challenges. These sections in the Seminar Extensions of this handbook explain the minor alterations necessary to make diverse learners comfortable and productive while learning in the same instructional unit.

In some cases, such as for a three-year spread in the traditional grade levels for students in a multiage environment, you may need to use two levels of the program. Even then, the skills and concepts overlap so that many lessons can productively accommodate all learners.

The student Practice Books provide another opportunity to accommodate follow-up for students. Use the books for independent practice. Then extend learning for selected students with the "apple" activity on the bottom of every practice page.

This program provides an infrastructure for a spelling curriculum in a classroom with traditional student groups or in a multiage classroom. With this scaffolding, you customize the program your way to make every child a speller.

Teaching Spelling Using the Sourcebooks for Levels 1, 7, and 8

The Sourcebook Series provides the infrastructure for creating a spelling curriculum, organized by grade level, 1–8. Levels 1, 7, and 8 vary slightly from Levels 2–6. Here are the differences.

Level 1

Most first-grade teachers implement the Sourcebook program about two to three months into the school year. Prior to that, students can be engaged in the spelling and word skill activities that initiate the Level 1 student Practice Book. Although the Practice Books are optional, these activities provide readiness for spelling if existing programs in reading and language are not sufficiently accommodating the learners. Forty-eight lessons precede the practice that complements each Sourcebook unit.

In Level 1, there are 21 units. The units are different from the units in subsequent levels in which each unit consists of a skills module, Build Skills and Word Experiences, and a testing module, Assess Words and Skills. In Level 1, there are two skills units, followed by a testing unit.

There are 35 Core Words in Level 1. As students engage in the skill-building activities, these Core Words are expanded to hundreds of words and language-related experiences. For example, the Core Word *in* is the catalyst for students to use analogous thinking to spell bin, chin, fin, grin, kin, pin, shin, sin, skin, spin, thin, tin, win. Then students make the nouns plural (e.g., pins) and explore regular past tense verbs (e.g., grinned). They learn that verbs that end with one vowel and one consonant double the final consonant before adding *ed*. And then they find more verbs that behave the same way. Students develop word power by making the 35 Core Words into many more words, and at the same time they make discoveries about how their language works.

This strong word and language base is developed through the increased emphasis in Level 1 on the skill-building component of the program driven by each unit's Core Words. It forms the foundation for spelling and writing that is expanded in subsequent grades.

The Level 1 program further deviates from the Series norm with a far greater emphasis on literature tie-ins. Evidence shows that early experiences with literature clearly contribute to measurable growth in language skills. Literature, spelling, and writing form an ongoing threesome throughout the Level 1 program.

Levels 7 and 8

Most 7th and 8th grade teachers know their students need a spelling curriculum, but have little time and limited resources to provide one. The Sourcebooks for Levels 7 and 8 are designed to meet this challenge.

As with all other levels of the Series, the Sourcebooks are a *resource* for developing student proficiency in spelling and related language skills. All previously introduced essential spelling skills are revisited, such as the basic rules for adding prefixes and suffixes to base words and roots—a frequent cause of spelling errors if writers are uninformed regarding their use. Yet, these essentials are limited to one concept within each unit, a modification to reflect the diminished time available at these levels for spelling instruction.

Beyond spelling basics, Levels 7 and 8 integrate spelling study extensively with building word understandings. Exercise Express is expanded to include Replace It, a word-building synonym activity. There is great weight at these levels on Latin and Greek roots, etymologies, words with multiple meanings, often-confused words, and words borrowed from other languages—all adaptations to augment the vocabulary development that is integral in 7th and 8th grade English.

To aid the development of writing fluency, Build Skillful Writers provides extensive practice with usage, capitalization, punctuation, comparisons, and other elements of effective writing.

Proofreading strategies are extended to ensure that students demonstrate proofreading competence in writing, as well as on standardized spelling achievement tests—all of which utilize a proofreading and editing format.

Many English teachers also teach Social Studies, so a chronological presentation of American history snippets is the vehicle used on the blackline master Proofreading Tests at these levels. This ensures that students, regardless of the Social Studies focus in these grades, know and appreciate their American multicultural heritage. On these tests, students practice proofreading for errors in spelling, capitalization, usage, mechanics, punctuation, and meaning.

There are many ways to increase students' ability to write, but the most basic, and consequently the most often overlooked, is by improving their spelling. The Sourcebooks provide your source for teaching spelling for writing, beginning in Level 1 and expanding sequentially and cumulatively through Levels 7 and 8.

Rescue the Rabbit

Pixie Holbrook, a veteran teacher, says this is her students' all-time favorite spelling game! She calls it "Rescue the Rabbit." The game begins with Pixie drawing a cartoon rabbit on the chalkboard as students watch. "This," she says, "is my friend, Fred." Letter blanks are drawn under the rabbit to represent the letters in the word to be spelled. Students take turns guessing the letters. Pixie reminds her students that every word has at least one vowel to encourage them to begin by selecting vowel letters.

With each incorrect guess, a small part of Fred is erased, such as one floppy ear or one of his two big teeth. Students gasp as Fred slowly disappears, one little bit at a time. When the word is discovered, the winning student steps up to the chalkboard and "rescues" the rabbit by redrawing the missing parts. Students must remember all the details as Fred is redrawn. Play continues with another word.

Mr. Pickyfood

Write on the chalkboard LIKES and DOESN'T LIKE. Introduce Mr. Pickyfood as a man who eats only what he likes. In the LIKES column, write peas, popcorn, and pumpkin pie. In the DOESN'T LIKE column, write jam, beans, and bread. Ask students to suggest a food Mr. Pickyfood likes. If the food begins with *p*, add it to the LIKES column. All other words go in the DOESN'T LIKE list. The object of the game is to discover the reason for Mr. Pickyfood's pickiness. (He only likes food that begins with *p*.)

Play Mr. Pickyfood using other reasons for his pickiness, such as foods with long *e*, double letters, or five letters. Mr. Pickyfood's picky cousins—Mr. Pickypack (travel items), Miss Pickywear (clothes), Mrs. Pickypet (animals)—continue the fun.

At the Races

Bonnie McClelland's Indiana students like this spelling game. Bonnie makes racetracks by cutting four long construction paper strips of equal length, each in a different color. She divides each track into spaces so that each track has fifteen or so spaces of various lengths. The racetracks are placed on a bulletin board.

The class is divided into four teams. Each team is identified by the color of its track. Teams make a paper race car and pin it just outside the first space on their track. Play begins with a "driver" from each team coming forward to sit in a "driver's seat"—desks used for this purpose. Then they are asked to write a word. Bonnie uses small chalkboards or paper for this activity. She also expects each member of the "pit crew"—the other members of each team—to write the word. Then she writes the word on the chalkboard. Students check their work. Each driver who spells the word correctly may advance his or her team's race car one space. The race continues, sometimes over several days. The first team to the finish line wins!

Connect the Dots

Provide each pair of students with a game sheet. The players need paper, pencil, and a word source (a student's individualized list of spelling words recorded in his/her Spelling Notebook, a list of review Core Words).

The first player selects a word, pronounces it, and uses it in a short context sentence to confirm its meaning. The other player writes the word. Then the players check the spelling of the word. If the word is spelled correctly, that player may connect two dots on the game sheet. Roles reverse and play continues.

The object of the game is to draw the last line to form a square on the game sheet and earn the number of points in the square. The player forming a square writes his/her initials in the square. The player with the most points at the end of the game wins!

```
· — · — · ———— ·
 | 4 . 2 . 5 .
 · ——— ·
 . 1 | 3 . 2 .
 ·   | ·   ·   ·
 . 7 . 4 . 6 .
```

Spelling Squares

Provide each student with a game sheet with letters or letter groups written in the squares. Each player can have a different game sheet, or they can be the same. Students need a pencil and paper. The object of the game is to list as many words as possible using the letters in the boxes. Words can be made by using letters in adjacent boxes only. Any letter can be doubled. Spelling Squares can also be played in cooperative learning groups or as a brainstorming game for the whole class.

N	I	D
ER	E	O
S	T	ED

DINNER   TEST
DIET   DINE
DOTTED   TEN
NEST   DOTS
TOE   SET   etc.

Grid Activities

Use grid paper to make word games. Students like to make word pyramids. They write a short word at the top of their grid. Then they write words under it, each progressively longer, forming a symmetric pyramid. If students begin with a one-letter word, their next word is a three-letter word, then a five-letter word, etc. If students begin with a two-letter word, their next word is a four-letter word, progressing toward the bottom of the paper. Then the letters can be traced in crayon to make colorful word pyramids. See Visual Skills for additional activities...

SUCH AS WORD SEARCH GAMES —

Modified Spelling Bee

Dan Anderson modified the spelling bee so that his students who needed the practice most would not be eliminated from play, as is the case with the customary version. Dan begins by writing words he wants to reinforce on small word cards with a context sentence on the back to confirm the meaning of the words, about twice as many cards as players. Then he divides his class into two teams of equal spelling ability.

The first player on the starting team selects a card, calls out the word, and reads it in the context sentence. The first player on the opposite team goes to the chalkboard and writes the word. Using the touch-each-letter procedure of the Word Preview, the players check the spelling. If the word is spelled correctly, the word card is eliminated from the game. If the word is misspelled, it is written correctly, erased, and the word card is returned to the pile.

Players are never eliminated from Dan's game, only word cards. The first team to eliminate the opposite team's cards is the winner.

> State, regional, and national spelling bee competitions are fine! Identify students who can perform well in these events. Provide after-school practice to perfect their skills. Provide as much extracurricular support for these academic teams as you do for your athletic teams.

All in the Family

Divide students into cooperative learning groups, each with paper and pencil. The teacher begins the game by calling out a current or review Core Word. The first player in each group writes the word. The paper and pencil is passed to the next member of the group and a derivative of the word is written. Each successive player writes a derivative until the group can think of no more, or until time is up (about three minutes). One point is awarded for the correct spelling of the base word and each of the derivatives. The group with the most points at the end of the game wins, or the whole class wins a prize when the point total for all groups combined reaches a certain number.

Spelling Baseball

Prepare for the game by arranging the classroom to accommodate a "baseball diamond"—three bases and home plate. Write review Core Words on cards, each with   a short context sentence that confirms the meaning of the word. Divide players into two teams. Determine the number of innings.

The first team sends their first player "to bat." The first player on the opposite team "pitches" a word from the set of cards to the batter. The batter writes the word on the chalkboard. The word is checked for spelling. If it is correct, the batter advances to first base and the second batter continues the game with the second player on the opposite team assuming the role of pitcher.

If a batter misses a word, it is an "out." Three outs and the opposite team is at bat. Points are scored when players cross home plate—they advance one base each time a word is spelled correctly. Continue through the last inning.

Prefix/Suffix Boxes

Prepare a box divided into nine equal boxes and make copies for future use. For Prefix Boxes, label each row with a different prefix. Label each column with a letter. The students fill in the boxes using words with the appropriate prefix and ending with the appropriate letter. For Suffix Boxes, label each row with a letter and each column with a suffix. Students fill in the boxes using words with the appropriate beginning letter and ending with the appropriate suffix. Have students share their games to make a cumulative list of correct responses for each box.

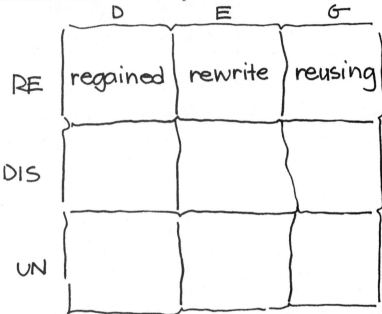

	D	E	G
RE	regained	rewrite	reusing
DIS			
UN			

Word Maker

Choose a seven-letter word (*reading*). The word maker writes a three-letter word on the chalkboard as a clue. The clue words consists of letters in any order taken from *reading* (*rid*). Students take turns writing words on the board to guess the word maker's word. If the word is not discovered, write a four-letter clue word (*grin*). Then a five-letter clue word is written (*grade*), and so on until the word is discovered.

Word Fun

Have students research the following and create ongoing charts for words collected:
- What are the longest words students can find?
- What words begin and end with the same letter? (*arena, edge, gang, hearth*)
- What words begin and end with consecutive letters? (*card, date, elf, frog, growth*)
- What words have the same letter occurring twice, but not together and not at the beginning or the end? (*engage, meter, thighs, civil*)
- What words with five or more letters use only the first or second half of the alphabet? (*blade, rusty, worst*)

Play *Plus One* in which each consecutive word uses the letters of the previous word plus one more (*he, she, hers, share, hearts, shatter*).

Play *Words in Words* in which students write words that can be spelled using the letters in a given word (*material: meat, team, tile, alarm*).

Why do students spell well on a word-list test but cannot spell the same words correctly in everyday writing? Why aren't we getting the results we want? Because...

Customary programs assign a weekly spelling list and rely heavily on memorization for mastery.
Why should we rely on memorization, the lowest level of learning, rather than long-term mastery? We know from our own experience it doesn't work for most students.

With the Sitton methodology, spelling instruction is not an assigned list of words. Word work includes higher-level thinking skills that help students form a foundation for how all words work— this is a reading curriculum instructional model, but without the same time investment. How well would students transfer reading words to their everyday reading tasks if reading instruction was a list of assigned words to be memorized for a weekly graded test?

Customary programs give out the answers to the test before the test is given.
If students have the answers to the test, they may only study the answers the night before so that they will know the answers just for the test. The test, then, tests students' (or parents') commitment to study the words for the test, and their ability to recall the spellings just for the test—short-term memory of the words is tested. Experience reveals that often when students study words just for a test, they forget the spellings soon after the test.

Wait! If we were to give out the answers to the math test the night before the test, we'd never know whether the students could do the math!

With the Sitton methodology, students do not have access to the exact words for any one test, although they can be given a copy of the Core Words list that identifies all words that are tested throughout the school year at that grade. The test, then, tests students' mastery of words. Words not yet mastered become a student's Spelling Words, targeted for study, and later retested on subsequent tests. The tests systematically recycle words from all previous grades.

Customary programs give students spelling words to study that do not occur as often as other words in everyday writing.
If we want to see better spelling in writing, students need to learn the words they use in everyday writing.

With the Sitton methodology, the words targeted for mastery are a research-based list of the highest-frequency writing words, a list of over 90% of all words adults need in their everyday writing. Yet, students learn still more words through their engagement in word-building activities.

Customary programs provide a single opportunity to learn important words—the week they're on the list.
Most students do not learn for a lifetime something they've studied once.

With the Sitton methodology, there are ongoing opportunities to revisit the same skills and words. There are skill tests and word tests—formative assessments that gather information about what students know and do not know. Then study is targeted to the skills and words that students need to learn.

Customary programs reward performance on one graded word-list test each week.
What we grade sends a strong message to students, identifying what we think is important. If our goal is transfer of words to writing, yet we give students their grade based on a word-list test before that goal is reached, the logical result is students who lack interest and motivation to transfer words to writing.

With the Sitton methodology, students rehearse for real-world use of spelling. Students discover that their ability to transfer an increasing number of high-use words into their everyday writing figures into their grade.

Customary programs teach some students they're spelling failures, and teach some students they're exemplary spellers—when neither is true.

Repeated spelling test failures may convince struggling students they cannot spell, so—indeed, they think they cannot spell. Once convinced, teaching spelling becomes a challenge—how do you teach students to do something that we've already convinced them they cannot do? Further, students who are capable of memorizing words just for a test (those who score well but fail to transfer words to writing) receive the message that they're good spellers. In fact, they may not be.

With the Sitton methodology, students who struggle are not failed, but given the time they need to succeed with repeated exposures to words and skills. Even for tests, minor modifications keep students who struggle with spelling on track with the class, feeling successful and making progress. For students who would have scored well on customary word-list tests, they learn that spellings must be learned forever, not just for a test. The Sitton methodology challenges these students with higher expectations and making discoveries about how our language system works.

Customary programs tell students to study spelling words and to proofread but don't teach them how.

It is important to remember that instruction counts. If students have been taught the how-to skills for success on a task, then the task provides an opportunity for them to apply the skills and be more successful than if they had not been taught the how-to skills.

With the Sitton methodology, students learn how to spell and proofread, and apply those skills routinely every day.

Customary programs often teach spelling as a subject apart from other language skills.

Because language learning has skills common to all, if students make the connections, students' language learning would benefit.

With the Sitton methodology, spelling and word skills are fully integrated with all language learning, particularly reading and writing. Simplistically, reading (decoding) teaches students how to look at letters and say the sounds, while spelling (encoding) teaches students to hear sounds and write the letters. Vocabulary building, too, is an essential element of both a reading and spelling curriculum. The Sitton methodology combines spelling, word skills, and writing so that students benefit from the connections the approach helps them make.

Customary programs use a one-size-fits-all spelling approach, because differentiating is too time consuming.

Different students have different needs, but common sense also dictates that there is only so much time to provide for those differences. Yet, if students could have instruction and practice on their level, student achievement increases.

With the Sitton methodology, differentiating is practical and time effective. Teachers select skill-building activities from a menu that offers choices of varying difficulty. The formative word tests provide a differentiated list of spelling words that require no additional teacher effort to retest because all words are automatically recycled for retesting to indicate progress. Further, this test can be easily modified for students who struggle so that they can participate with the class. And a more difficult test is also included in each unit for students who need challenge.

Customary programs do not rely on or apply the research regarding the benefits of formative assessment.

Common sense and best practices tell us that instruction is better when we teach students what they need to learn rather than whatever comes next in a program.

With the Sitton methodology, formative tests in every unit gather information on student progress to tell teachers what students have yet to learn. For example, the Skill Test reveals how well students are mastering the application of essential skills, and the Cloze Story Word Test and the Sentence Dictation Test indicate students' ability to spell essential words. Teachers can use this information to target instruction and practice to students' needs.

APPLESEED
E-newsletter

APPLESEED IDEA CENTER

Sign up for the complimentary *Appleseed* e-newsletter at www.sittonspelling.com. You'll receive three issues per year—November, January, and March. Peruse and print archived issues. Here's some of what you'll find—

Word-Skill Activities

- "Thanksgiving" word-making activities (11/05)
- "Valentine" word-skill activities (01/06)
- Multiple-meaning word activities (03/06)
- "Welcome back" word-making activities (08/06)
- Tips for a Thanksgiving word wall (11/06)
- Compound word activities (01/07)
- Phonics activities with the letters *ch* (03/07)

Sourcebook Teaching Tips

- Ideas for using the Core Words blackline master (11/05)
- Sort-It—a powerful word-skill and cognitive activity (11/05)
- A how-to guide for selecting Sourcebook activities (01/06)
- Suggestions for using the Sourcebook with Special Ed students (01/06)
- Getting parents involved (03/06)
- A word-collection strategy (03/06)
- What is a Core Word? What is a Priority Word? (11/06)
- Eight ways to get Sourcebook teaching questions answered (11/06)
- Using the Sourcebooks to teach vocabulary (01/07)
- How to give a Cloze Story Word Test (01/07)
- Value of giving the (5-minute) Word Preview (03/07)

Ask Sitton (formerly Ask Rebecca)

- How will students new to the program learn words and skills from previous levels? (11/05)
- What is the source for the Spelling Words? How do students study and learn them? (01/06)
- How does the Sourcebook methodology work with students out of the mainstream—very capable spellers and students who struggle with spelling? (01/06)
- Why focus on high-frequency words instead of word patterns? (03/06)
- What suggestions do you have for students who routinely miss more than half the words on the Cloze Story Word Test? (11/06)
- How do the skills taught in the Sourcebook tie to a student's Spelling Words? (11/06)
- Why is run a 3rd grade word? (01/07)
- How is recordkeeping handled for the Spelling Words? (03/07)
- How do the Sourcebooks empower my curriculum decisions? (03/07)

What's Current?

- Using mini-lessons to teach to state standards (11/05)
- Using graphic organizers to teach spelling (01/06)
- Differentiation—what, why, how (01/06)
- Using a reading model to teach spelling (03/06)
- What counts as evidence-based instruction? (03/06)
- Visualizing—a research-based strategy for learning to spell and learning to read (11/06)
- Best practice instruction: Teaching students how (01/07)
- Constructing meaning through reading and writing (01/07)
- ELL challenges: How can vocabulary-building meet the challenge? (03/07)
- No carryover? Four questions and four answers (03/07)

SITTON SPELLING AND WORD SKILLS®
Rebecca Sitton

by Beth Davis

Introduction

Through the years, spelling has often been viewed as the poor sister of the language arts and as such has not experienced the variety of instructional methods that have characterized the teaching of reading and writing (Adams, 1991). With the advent of spell check on computers, the impetus to seek research-based strategies for effective spelling teaching is even less of a priority although spelling has been the focus of a number of researchers -- Bear and Templeton (1998), Ehri (1992), Horn (1969), Peters (1985), Zutell (1996), and others.

In many cases, spelling has been taught in a nearly identical fashion in most elementary classrooms. Teachers identify a base of words at the beginning of each week, administer a pretest, have children practice the words during the week, and test the words on Friday. Perhaps once a month or at the end of a unit, the Friday test will include words from the previous weeks. Identifying common phonic elements, practicing writing the words with various exercises during the week, and memorizing are the key learning strategies.

Sitton Spelling and Word Skills® has as its primary goal "forever spellers" who "learn to spell for writing" (Sourcebook, Level 1, p. vii) rather than the Friday test goal. Emphasizing instruction tailored to: individual needs; the importance of explicit, direct teaching; proofreading and self checking; the central role of word study; the recycling of skills; using the known to discover the unknown; and the bond between spelling and writing, this spelling program culls best practices from the research into a multifaceted program that bolsters and enriches the entire classroom language arts curriculum.

Sitton Spelling and Word Skills® has as its primary goal "forever spellers" who "learn to spell for writing" rather than the Friday test goal. Emphasizing instruction tailored to: individual needs; the importance of explicit, direct teaching; proofreading and self checking; the central role of word study; the recycling of skills; using the known to discover the unknown; and the bond between spelling and writing, this spelling program culls best practices into a multifaceted program that bolsters and enriches the entire classroom language arts curriculum.

Direct, explicit instruction, shown to be important for spelling acquisition (Peters, 1985; Spiegel, R.T., 1992; Zutell, 1996; Templeton and Morris, 1999) is a hallmark of this program where the teacher plays a very active and central role. Peters (1985) speaks of the teacher's task as that of directing students' attention to 'catch' spelling. As the "expert other" (Vygotsky, 1978), the teacher assists students at that "zone of proximal development" between the skills they have attained and those presenting difficulty. What the teacher assists with soon becomes an independent skill, therein establishing a new zone. This scaffolding of instruction requires not only the explicit teaching found at all levels of *Sitton Spelling and Word Skills*® but the ability to differentiate instruction according to need as well. The Sourcebooks and Practice Books, with their myriad of activities, skills and assessment techniques, both allow and actively encourage teachers to individualize.

Word Choice

Sitton Spelling and Word Skills® utilizes 1200 Core Words selected for their frequency of use in writing. These represent and exceed the 1000 word number that has been identified to make up 90% of the words used in routine written communication (Sipe, p. 75, 2003). Thomas Horn in 1969 wrote, "It is very probable that spelling ability is best developed and maintained in the long run through stimulation of, and careful attention to, the writing that children do. On the other hand, there is as yet no field-tested substitute for direct instruction on the basic core of high-frequency words needed in child and adult writing"(p. 1285).

The teaching units in the 8 levels of the program all follow a similar format. All begin with the Word Preview. Here the teacher introduces the Core Words for the unit. The Core Words are familiar words that students already can read. "Children should not be expected to correctly spell words they can not read or words they rarely hear or use" (Zutell, R.T. p. 609, 1990). The Core Words are not necessarily the students' spelling words but rather the words are used as a springboard to build essential skills and concepts in each unit.

Visual Skills and Automaticity

The Word Preview uses these Core Words to build visual skills needed for good spelling and proofreading and that are key to making students lifelong spellers. The importance of visual skills was revealed in a large-scale research study of spelling and handwriting by Peters in 1970 (Peters, 1991). Documenting children's spelling progress and teaching strategies from a total age group of a local district's primary school population throughout their last two primary school years, "one of the findings most relevant to the teaching of spelling was that the most significant factor was visual perception of word form", a finding repeatedly confirmed since (p. 220). Adams (1991) cites research "that seeing a word in print is not just superior to hearing it spelled but is an extremely powerful and effective means of acquiring its spelling" (p. 396). The second important factor was swift, legible handwriting, leading Peters to conclude that " … spelling is primarily a visuo-motor activity" (p. 220) and that practice in writing letter sequences is a critical aspect of spelling acquisition.

The *Sitton Spelling and Word Skills*® Sourcebooks provide direct, explicit instruction that develops students' abilities to picture the sequential letters of a familiar word from their long-term memory bank and develop the proofreading skills to verify their efforts. Students

are asked to carefully check their written production of each sequential letter in a word as well as self-correct in a rewrite. "Spelling is 'caught'" through the child's developing forms of imagery and serial reconstructions and, as a consequence of this becoming accustomed to the probability of letter sequences occurring" (Peters, p. 37, 1985). Peters describes spelling as a type of grammar in which the occurrence of letter strings/combinations ranges from highly likely, to likely, and on through impossible. The continual repetition throughout the Word Preview helps to develop automatic attention to the written word, its letter string(s), and whether it "looks right"; that is, a proofreading state of mind.

Samuels (1979) speaks of automaticity as action without conscious effort. As students reread what they have written, they are primed from the repetitive visual training of the Word Preview to have an awareness of words not looking right and to know the steps available to them for correcting. In checking their spelling attempts with the help of a reference, students circle only what is incorrect in the word, helping them to zero in on what needs correcting. "Expert spellers develop a visual memory for words…

The Word Preview uses Core Words to build visual skills needed for good spelling and proofreading and that are key to making students lifelong spellers.

99

Word study makes an important contribution to learning to spell correctly. "What students store in memory about specific words' spellings is regulated in part by what they know about the general system. Learners who lack the knowledge are left with rote memorization which takes longer and is more easily forgotten."

Having kids correct their own errors immediately seems to aid their memory" (Gentry, 1987). The skills taught in the Word Preview help students to avoid careless errors of known words in their every day writing thereby encouraging writing fluency.

The Core Words used in the Word Preview to develop visual skills are then used in the second activity in each of the teaching units, the Exercise Express. These six optional activities may be used at any time once the students are familiar with what is expected. These activities, developing from the Core Words, (stretching simple sentences; finishing sentence starters; fixing errors in sentences; word sorts; adding words to an identified pattern; and finding words to add to a pattern) teach students processes and strategies for examining and thinking about words and their application in writing (Sourcebook, Level 1, p. 152).

Word Study

Word study makes an important contribution to learning to spell correctly. "What students store in memory about specific words' spellings is regulated in part by

what they know about the general system. Learners who lack the knowledge are left with rote memorization which takes longer and is more easily forgotten" (Ehri, p. 308, 1992). Funnell (1992) offers an equally compelling need for word study. She posits that being able to read a word is not a guarantee that one can spell the word or even necessarily detect misspellings, especially if the appropriate letters are present but incorrectly ordered. Good spellers require a more complete orthographic description where letter position is critical. Word study examines the complete orthographic makeup of words and word parts and helps to cement visual recognition and memory of the appropriate letter strings.

Word study, further, acknowledges the role of meaning and grammar in spelling. "An effective word study program provides students with many formal and informal opportunities to examine words carefully, explore their orthographic forms in relation to their meanings and uses, and develop reliable and efficient strategies for independent word learning" (Zutell, p. 107, 1996). It integrates the various aspects of language—phonics, word structure, word meaning, and sentence structure. Words may be looked at in isolation but they are taken from and returned to written context. Good teaching helps students 'catch' the conventions that each of these aspects of language impose on word spellings.

Word study is meant to follow the instructional needs of students at the developmental stages at which research has suggested children acquire spelling skill (Bear and Templeton, 1998; Bear et al 2000; Ehri, 1997). In harmony with their growth in reading and writing, students become more sophisticated in their knowledge of the information that spelling represents—alphabetic (letter sound left to right matching), pattern (vowel chunks and syllable groupings), and meaning (constancy of spelling despite variant sound as in *prefer/preference*; difference in spelling and meaning with constancy of sound as in *bear, bare*). As students move through these stages, from prephonemic or emergent, to letter name-alphabetic, to within word pattern, to syllables and affixes, to derivational relations (Bear et al, 2000), word study instruction and activities should be chosen to cement and advance the particulars of growing spelling usage that students show they are capable of understanding.

In the Seeds for Sowing Skills section, word study builds skills and concepts. The Seeds for Sowing Skills section includes a number of suggestions for instruction in appropriate concepts. Under each concept is a menu of activities usually at varying levels of challenge. The Sourcebooks suggest that teachers choose activities that coordinate with the total language curriculum for the class and are appropriate for some or all of the students. It is not expected that every activity will be used. At the same time, it does not matter if all of the students are exposed to each concept in a unit. That is because the concepts are revisited again and again throughout the Sourcebooks.

Spiraling, Deepening, and Extending Skills and Concepts

Spiraling skills allows the teacher to individualize instruction so that students have the readiness to benefit. In addition, students who are not as able as others to 'catch' instruction the first time around are given many opportunities to achieve mastery. A scope and sequence chart found at the end of each Sourcebook lists the skills and concepts that comprise the program and where they may be found. Skills

Teachers choose Sourcebook activities that coordinate with the total language curriculum for the class and are appropriate for some or all of the students. Extensive instructional options are offered for teacher selection based on their students' needs so effectiveness is not based on using every activity.

are not limited strictly to spelling and cover the whole range of hearing, speaking, reading, writing, and thinking.

Zutell (1996) concurs with many of the findings that have emerged from the developmental approach to spelling described above from which it is recognized that a progressive understanding of the ways in which words 'work' is crucial to spelling acquisition. Patterns that are discovered first in familiar words are then found and related to a broadening expansion of less familiar words. Concept building exercises in the Sourcebooks begin with the familiar Core Words and cull like patterns from numbers of oral and written sources to which students are exposed, as they learn to relate the known to the unknown. Learning by analogy expands their reading and meaning vocabularies along with their spelling progress. Starting at the early levels this may be seen as they build words by adding letters to known Core Words that are also rimes such as *and*, resulting in possibilities as simple as *band* or progressively difficult as *strand* or *understand*. Using the Core Words the teacher is able to help students generate hundreds of words from the 37 high frequency

rimes cited in professional texts (Adams, 1990; Cunningham, 2000).

At Level 6, beginning with the Core Word *scale* with its silent e, students look at other words exhibiting silent letters, moving from simpler "gn" words like *sign,* to the more difficult words like *campaign* and *align,* and on to more difficult silent letters like the "l" in *salmon*. In addition they learn about word origins, such as, that silent letters in words such as *yacht* are the result of borrowings from other languages (p.155). Adding affixes to Core Words enables instruction not only about vocabulary but plurals, possessives, and comparatives, as well as how root meanings trump spelling over sound (Bear and Templeton, 1998; Bear et al, 2000). Core Words also generate homophones and homographs.

Word study concepts are often taught and practiced with word sorts. By comparing, contrasting, and classifying patterns within words, students reinforce concepts about how words work, about their structure and the importance of letter sequence and how these inform both sound and meaning (Templeton and Morris, 1999). Word sorts comply with Zutell's conviction that the best teaching and practice activities provide numerous opportunities for students to write the applicable words. As important, however, are the opportunities they present that encourage students to discover word relationships and thereby "develop strategies for remembering the difficult parts" (Zutell, p. 103, 1996).

The Exercise Express activities, Sort It, Add It, and Find It, which work on classifying patterns, are activities where Core Words and the skills students have been working with may be practiced. These activities, like the skill building activities, contribute to the atmosphere of developmental and differentiated instruction. There are many choices for activity procedures. For example, they may be assigned as a whole class, small group, partner, or individual activity, or as homework. Within any of those choices, the demands or expectations may differ for some or all students. It is the teacher's decision as to which activities in both the Exercise Express and the Seeds for Sowing Skills sections are used, as well as when and how. "To plan effective instruction, the teacher must know not only where the student presently is, but where he or she needs to go next" (Templeton and Morris, p. 111, 1999).

Spelling to Write, Writing to Spell

Researchers who focus on effective spelling instruction (Peters, 1985; Wilde, 1990; Templeton, 1999) speak about spelling as more than knowing the words for the Friday test. It is also in the writing that students do in and out of class that spelling knowledge needs to show. "The real foundation for spelling is frequent writing" (Gentry, p. 33, 1987). Many of the activities in the Exercise Express are aimed at expanding students' opportunities for writing where the transfer of spelling skills may be observed. In Stretch It, students respond to a series of guidewords to expand sentences. Sentence starters are used for the activity Finish It. Both of these, in addition to Fix It where sentences are given for error revision, have students apply the proofreading skills taught and practiced with the Word Preview. The success that students achieve when they are able to self-correct their writing develops a self-confidence that results in expanding writing output (Peters, 1985).

Many of the activities... are aimed at expanding students' opportunities for writing where the transfer of spelling skills may be observed.

All of the skill building teaching and practice in the Sourcebooks, the visual, as well as the word study components, have as its primary goal students who spell correctly and fluently in whatever writing they do. The ability to proofread, therefore, is of primary importance. Although proofreading is taught and practiced with the Word Preview and practiced further in Exercise Express activities, every unit also includes a section titled Priority Words. The focus of this section is to proofread for what are identified in the Sourcebook as Priority Words, the highest frequency words for which correct spelling is always expected in students' writing. Referred to as "no excuses" words, "they designate a minimum competency for spelling accountability" (Sourcebook Level 1, p.164).

Students are given a Priority Word list which is continually growing. They are responsible, with the help of a provided spelling reference, for proofreading all of their work, regardless of subject, to ensure that they spell these words accurately every time. Because students are encouraged to write right from the beginning, invented spelling is the norm for students in early levels. Proofreading for a growing list of Priority Words helps students to recognize that over time all words need to be spelled correctly, that spelling counts. The skills they are gaining from the Word Preview (visual) and Seeds for Sowing Skills (word study) provide further encouragement. All along the way, other words may be added to individual lists when appropriate. Proofreading time is provided in class for writing assignments, and once a week the teacher collects and checks a piece of everyday writing. Any errors are noted and the papers are returned to the students to correct.

Funnell's research (1992), discussed on page 3, explains why even some students who read well may fail to recognize their misspellings if they have not fully learned the spelling of a word, that is, the complete linear description of its letter identities. Proofreading with *Sitton Spelling and Word Skills*™ gives students the Priority Word lists, their individual spelling lists, word walls—a number of sources against which students may match their written words letter for letter. Griffith and Leavell (1995) stress the importance of having these kinds of resources available in the classroom to help students apply proofreading skills.

Proofreading for a growing list of Priority Words helps students to recognize that over time all words need to be spelled correctly, that spelling counts.

Assessment

Informal assessment of Priority Words occurs with the classroom writing that students do. Informal assessment of an essential visual, language, and/or word study skill, which has been the focus of the Word Preview, Exercise Express, and Seeds for Sowing Skills sections of each unit occurs in the section called Test Ready. The activities found there, one for school and one for home, zero in on the skill, which will be formally tested in the upcoming Skill Test section. While the teacher chooses which activities to use for which students in the Exercise Express and Seeds for Sowing Skills sections, the Test Ready activities are intended for all of the students in a class. Differentiation may come in the grouping configurations chosen. The home activity may be done at school for some or all children. For the home tasks, black line masters are provided.

More formal assessment of the words and skills taught throughout the Sourcebooks occurs in the second part of each unit, which is called Assess Words and Skills. The first assessment, the Word Test, is a cloze-story or story context in which the Core Words have been deleted. Bear and Templeton (1998) advocate working with words outside of

context and then returning the words back to a context. In addition to the meaning assistance that the context may convey, it is within the visual field of context that students should be demonstrating their proficiency. Students do not pre-study the words for the Word Test, but they have been working with some of them throughout the unit, and with others in previous units. Any of the words misspelled here become their individual spelling words for home and school study. The program provides a number of resources for them to record their personal study lists of spelling words. Each subsequent Word Test, in addition to using the Core Words introduced in the unit, draws from the bank of previous Core Words. Thus the words recycle numerous times through the Word Tests. This test-study-test format recommended in the research on spelling assessment (Allred, 1984; Gentry, 1990) gives students many opportunities for retesting to achieve mastery and to progress at their appropriate developmental level. The teacher, noting which words are troublesome for which students, structures reteaching and practice with the word study strategy—read, spell, cover, print, proofread (Peters, 1985; Schlagal, 1998; Bear, 2000), as well as through the numerous activity opportunities

Students do not pre-study the words for the Word Test per se, but they have been working with some of them throughout the unit, and with others in previous units. Any of the words misspelled in the Word Test become their individual spelling words for home and school study.

105

previously cited. Since many of the words tested are also Priority Words that must always be spelled correctly, informal assessment, proofreading, and self-correcting is ongoing.

Following the Word Test is the Skill Test. It assesses the particular skill that has been the focus of the Test Ready section. Because the Sourcebooks promote both visual and word study skills as crucial ingredients for spelling success, it is important to assess students' progress in retaining these language skills and concepts. For students who have trouble with the skill, the Test Ready exercises may be revisited. The skill building and practice sections of the units will recycle the skill multiple times, and there will be numerous assessment opportunities for students to demonstrate progress/mastery.

An optional assessment choice is the Sentence Dictation Test. This test is made up of sentences relating to one another, forming a short story and is used for students needing more practice or challenge, again testing many of the Core Words. This provides not only additional confirmation of the Word Test findings but information on capitalization and punctuation as well. Like the Word Test, the Sentence Dictation Test assesses

long-term mastery. Words that are missed are recorded with their other spelling words on their "words to learn" sheet or spelling notebooks.

In addition, at Levels 5 through 8, a Proofreading Test is administered to all students. The test allows students to practice following directions and gaining familiarity with the format of standardized tests. Students are given the editing tasks of finding and/or correcting spelling and/or punctuation. The importance of proofreading and editing skills in *Sitton Spelling and Word Skills®* has been documented above. Wilde (1990) bemoans the fact that teachers often return student papers having circled or corrected spelling and punctuation errors rather than seeking to encourage independent proofreading, a task for which they may have had little or no instruction. "Students need, from the beginning, [age appropriate] guidance in how to produce a polished final draft, which is presumably the ultimate goal of spelling instruction" (pp. 285–86). Proofreading skills are significantly addressed in all of the units from Level 1 on, especially in the Practice Books, where there is a proofreading practice page for each corresponding unit. Although the skills are assessed informally in all student work, the Proofreading

Test at levels 5 through 8 allows the teacher a more focused evaluation of how well students are progressing with these skills and where more practice may be indicated.

Other assessments for *Sitton Spelling and Word Skills®* include achievement tests administered at three points during the year. Like with the Word Test, a cloze-story format is used. Black line masters are used for all of the Word, Skill, and Proofreading Tests, facilitating record keeping for the teacher.

The Home-School Connection

Educators, as a rule, view the home-school connection as a desirable component of an effective literacy program (Cooper, 2000; Cunningham, P. et al, 2000). It is important, however, that if parents are asked to provide home support, that they be given the tools they will need with which to participate (Padask, Rasinski, 2006). *Sitton Spelling and Word Skills®* seeks to include parents and keeps them informed about what is expected of their children in regard to spelling. Letters are sent home to parents explaining the ways in which they may help their children with take-home tasks, skill building exercises, proofreading papers, and words to learn. One of the parent letters

focuses on proofreading, including tips and activities they can do with their children. Priority Word lists accompany this letter and are continually updated. Bear et al. (2000) concur that parents should be encouraged to assist with spelling homework as "parents are typically firm believers in the importance of spelling because it is such a visible sign of literacy..." (p. 86).

Spelling Is a Language Art

The section called Relating to Literature, found in Level 1, underscores the basic premise that spelling is a skill that must be viewed in the context of a total language arts literacy program. Appropriate literature and writing experiences as well as follow-up activities help to highlight and expand the skill knowledge the students are learning in the program. Since Priority Words are high frequency words used repeatedly in reading and writing, immersion in both activities would be the logical reinforcement of the visuo-motor skills researchers such as M. L. Peters (1985, 1991) have found critical to acquiring accurate spelling. So too, literature and writing offers students opportunities to "assimilate new spelling and new vocabulary into memory" (Schlagal and Schlagal, p. 422, 1992) by relating to similar unfamiliar

Sitton Spelling and Word Skills® seeks to include parents and keeps them informed about what is expected of their children in regard to spelling.

words, understandings about letter patterns (*and, understand*) or meaning based spelling patterns (*sign, signify*) that they have learned with familiar words. Literature and writing also give continuing context for the additional phonics patterns, punctuation, homophones, vocabulary, affixes, hypothesizing, and other skills students are instructed in throughout the Sourcebooks. Peters' (1985) spelling research through the 1960s to 1970 revealed that spelling ability was best predicted by verbal ability, underscoring the benefits of language enrichment fostered through all of the language arts.

And the Standards Concur...

In 1996, the National Council of Teachers of English in partnership with the International Reading Association published Standards for the English Language Arts. The 12 standards identify the overarching goals for curriculum and instruction for the oral, written, and visual language skills and knowledge that students need. Beyond the skills and knowledge, however, the framers stress the need for students to know how to learn. "The conscious process of learning how to learn is an essential element in students' language arts education, and it forms a central theme in the standards (NCTE/IRA, 1996, p.7). Each unit of

the *Sitton Spelling and Word Skills*® Sourcebooks provides instruction in visual and proofreading skills, as well as the critical thinking skills (exercised through collection and analysis of words) needed to promote the discovery of spelling skills and concepts.

The specific standard 6 that stipulates that students apply knowledge of spelling conventions is only one of the standards addressed by the Sourcebooks. With their emphasis on applications in writing, the Sourcebooks attend to multiple standards. The specific behaviors appropriate for each of the 12 standards, however, have been spelled out in more detail according to grade level in the standards most states have adopted. Using a representative sampling of the states (CA, 1997; CO, 1995; MA, 2001; OH, 2001; WI, 1998), the more specific state standards call for students to use: progressively more conventional spelling in their edited writing as they learn to spell correctly: grade appropriate words; phonetically regular words as phonic elements (letter sounds, word parts) are taught; regularly used and high frequency words; words using common spelling generalizations (dropping *e*, doubling consonants, *y* words); and homophones, affixed words, multi-syllable words, and derivatives in higher grades.

In addition, students will use a variety of spelling strategies and will use resources (dictionaries, word walls, word lists) to monitor their spelling.

As shown, the Sourcebooks not only provide instruction in all the above but do so with immediate application in written work. The continual recycling of instruction and words, as well as the emphasis on proofreading, results in a greater likelihood that these standards will be easily met to produce fluent spellers.

Conclusion

It is the teacher who is the key to a successful spelling program. *Sitton Spelling and Word Skills®* assures success. This program recognizes that spelling is a skill that is acquired developmentally (Bear and Templeton, 1998; Bear et al 2000; Ehri, 1997) and that instruction must be developmentally rather than age or grade appropriate (Templeton and Morris, 1999). The Sourcebooks offer the teacher direct, explicit guidance for multilevel skill building instruction for differentiated groupings or teaching configurations. Evaluation both informal and formal is a part of every unit and informs the teacher as to which activities and skills are needed for every student. Teaching and evaluation of Core Words and skills recycle continually through each level allowing students to achieve mastery when they are developmentally ready. Pages of written instructions to the teacher are included for students with "special" needs at both ends so there need be no lack of challenge for the able or frustration for the slower learner. Explicit instruction and material is provided to the teacher for parent involvement. Students using *Sitton Spelling and Word Skills®* have every reason to become "lifelong spellers".

The Sourcebooks not only provide instruction but do so with immediate application in written work. The continual recycling of instruction and words as well as the emphasis on proofreading results in a greater likelihood that state standards will be easily met to produce fluent spellers.

Rebecca Sitton is the author of the popular *Sitton Spelling and Word Skills*® program. She began her career as a teacher in Oregon. Sitton was involved with regular education, special education, and curriculum and staff development.

In support of her spelling program, Sitton has traveled around the country giving seminars on spelling instruction. During her travels, she talks with classroom practitioners, keeping current on classroom issues and the needs of teachers and students. Sitton has developed a stellar reputation as a spelling authority. She was the spelling instructor for the Bureau of Education and Research for many years.

Sitton has also published language arts and spelling materials for preschool to adult students, covering both regular and special education needs.

Sitton holds degrees in Speech Pathology-Audiology and Education, an M.A. in Special Education, and certificates in Extreme Learning Problems, Early Childhood Education, and School Administration.

Beth G. Davis began her career as an elementary school teacher. She has been a Title 1 Evaluator, instructed tutors for School Volunteers for Boston, and has been a presenter at the Massachusetts Reading Association. She is the co-author of Elementary Reading: Strategies That Work (Allyn and Bacon, 1996) and the author of the Reteach and Practice Teacher Guides for EPS *Phonics PLUS* (Educators Publishing Service, 2006).

Davis is an Emerita Lecturer from Brandeis University, where she taught students from both Brandeis and Wellesley College for nearly 30 years. She received her BA from Smith College and her MEd in Reading from Boston College, where she also taught.

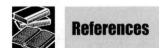

References

Adams, M. (1991). *Beginning to Read: Thinking and Learning about Print*. Cambridge, MA: The MIT Press.

Allred, R.(1984). *Spelling Trends, Content, and Methods. What Research says to the Teachers*. Washington, DC: National Education Association.

Bear, D.R. and Templeton, S. (1998). Explorations in developmental spelling: Foundations for learning and teaching phonics, spelling, and vocabulary. *The Reading Teacher*. 52, pp. 222–242.

Bear, Donald R., Marcia Invernizzi, Shane Templeton, and Francine Johnston (2000). Words Their Way: Word Study for Phonics, Vocabulary, and Spelling Instruction. Upper Saddle River, NJ: Prentice Hall.

California Department of Education (1997). English-Language Arts Content Standards for California Public Schools. http://www.cde.ca.gov/be/st/ss/engmain.asp

Colorado Department of Education (1995). www.cde.state.co.us/artemis/ed1/ED1202R341995INTERNET

Cooper, J. D. (2000). Literacy: Helping Children Construct Meaning. Boston: Houghton Mifflin Company.

Cunningham, P., Moore, S., Cunningham J., and Moore, D. (2000). *Reading and Writing in Elementary Classrooms: Strategies and Observations*. New York: Longman.

1992 Ehri, L. C. Review and commentary: Stages of spelling development. In S. Templeton & D. Bear (Eds.), *Development of Orthographic Knowledge and the Foundations of Literacy: A Memorial Festschrift for Edmund H. Henderson* (pp. 307–332). Hillsdale, N.J.: Erlbaum.

Ehri, L. C. (1997). Learning to read and learning to spell are one and the same, almost. In C. Perfetti, L. Rieban and, & M. Fatol (Eds.), *Learning to spell: Research, theory, and practice across the languages* (pp. 237-269), Mahwah, NJ: Erlbaum.

Griffith, P. and Leavell, J. (1995). There isn't much to say about spelling … or is there? *Childhood Education*, 72, pp. 84–90.

Funnell, Elaine (1992). On recognizing misspelled words. In Sterling and Robson (ed.) *Psychology, Spelling and Education*. Clevedon: Multilingual Matters Ltd., pp. 86–99.

Horn, T.D. (1969). Spelling. In R.L. Ebel (Ed.), *Encyclopedia of educational research* (4th ed., pp. 1282–1299). New York: Macmillan.

Massachusetts Department of Education (2001). Massachusetts English Language Arts Curriculum Framework. http://www.doe.mass.edu/frameworks/ela/0601.pdf

National Council of Teachers of English (1996). Standards for the English Language Arts. www.ncte.org/about/over/standards.

Ohio Department of Education (2001). English Language Arts Academic Content Standards. www.ode.state.oh.us/GD/Templates/Pages/ODE/ODEDefaultPage.aspx?page=1

Padak, N. and Rasinski, T. (2006). Home-school partnerships in literacy education: From rhetoric to reality. *The Reading Teacher*, 60, pp. 292–295.

Peters, M. L. (1992). Toward spelling autonomy. In Sterling and Robson (ed.) *Psychology, Spelling and Education*. Clevedon: Multilingual Matters Ltd., pp. 220–23.

Peters, M. L. (1985). *Spelling: Caught or Taught? A New Look*. London: Routledge and Kegan Paul.

Samuels, S. J. (1979). The method of repeated readings. *The Reading Teacher*, 32, 403–408.

Schlagal, B. and Trathen, W. (1998) American Spelling Instruction: What history tells us. *American Reading Forum Online Yearbook*, 18. http://www.americanreading forum.org

Schlagal, R. C. and Schlagal, J. H. (1992). The integral character of spelling: teaching strategies for multiple purposes. *Language Arts*, 69, pp. 418–25.

Sipe, Rebecca (2003). *They Still Can't Spell? Understanding and Supporting Challenged Spellers in Middle and High School*. Portsmouth NH: Heinemann.

Spiegel, Dixie Lee (1992). Blending whole language and systematic instruction. *The Reading Teacher*, 46, pp. 38–44.

Templeton, S. and Morris, D. (1999). Theory and Research into Practice: Questions teachers ask about spelling. *Reading Research Quarterly*, 34, pp. 102–112.

Vygotsky, L. (1978). *Mind in society: the development of higher psychological processes*. Cambridge, MA: Harvard University Press.

Wilde, S. (1990). A proposal for a new spelling curriculum. *The Elementary School Journal*, 90, pp. 275–290.

Wisconsin Department of Public Instruction (1998). English Language Arts-Standard B-Performance Standards. http://dpi.state.wi.us/standards/elasamp.html

Zutell, J. (1990). In Jongsma, K.S. Reading-spelling links. *The Reading Teacher*, 43, pp. 608–610.

Zutell, J. (1996). The Directed Spelling Thinking Activity: Providing an effective balance in word study instruction. *The Reading Teacher*, 50, pp. 98–108.

One Teacher's Approach...

Implementing Sitton Spelling and Word Skills®

Now we're using the Third Edition of the Series, but here is how it began. I was looking at my students' book reports, and for the thousandth time I circled misuse of *there*, *their*, and *they're*—and numerous other words my fifth graders should know. In our faculty meeting that morning, the district writing test results were announced. The news was disappointing—with points off for spelling errors and editing oversights, scores remained dismally low. What to do!

Then I noticed a Spelling Seminar flier posted in the office. It was Rebecca Sitton's workshop on how to increase students' spelling achievement, not just on tests, but in everyday writing. Too good to be true? Probably, but I attended anyway.

I had heard Rebecca Sitton speak several years before, and she made sense, but I never followed through with her ideas. This time, her message impacted me. I was excited! I saw the connections her approach has with what I'd been learning about brain research, learning styles, and differentiated instruction. Even though it was January, I ordered the Level 5 Spelling Sourcebook, Second Edition, and started. And it made a difference!

I shared my results with colleagues, so in the fall our whole school started the program. Everyone was willing to try, but there was considerable apprehension. There was no Friday Test! To use this program requires a new thought process for spelling, and anxieties surfaced as teachers struggled to understand. I assured my colleagues that there were tests, take-home word lists, and all the traditional skills in the new program—they're just arranged differently.

A prerequisite for some to begin was an ability to see the whole picture. But I encouraged them to *just start*. I assured them they'd "get it" later. I told them to jump in with Unit 1, even though the program was new to them and their students.

Before long, the new thought process began to usurp the old. Each teacher developed a comfortable routine, albeit slightly different. The program encourages flexibility. But, you asked me to describe what I do in my classroom, so here is what *I do*. Remember, I don't consider myself an expert, but having two years of experience with the program, I'm quite comfortable with the following routine.

Before I do any spelling with my students, there are some "getting ready" things I do:
- I acquaint parents—I send home the Introducing Spelling Blackline Master. If parents want more clarification, I send home a copy of the Overview, which is an introduction to the program. You can get this free introduction on DVD by calling 888-WE-SPELL or visiting www.epsbooks.com/sittonspelling. And it's OK to make copies. Further, I may invite parents to view the TUTOR ME Training® for Parents CD-ROM. Once they see how sensible the program is, they're supporters.
- I make copies of other blackline masters I've decided to use, such as—
  * Words to Learn (kids use one copy in every unit) and Ideas for Word Study (another parent letter). I run these two off back-to-back. They're in the back of the Sourcebook.

Frustration with my students' spelling was the catalyst that introduced me to Rebecca Sitton's approach to teaching spelling.

A different way of thinking about spelling is necessary with this approach.

First things first.

Parent support is essential.

Prepare the blackline masters.

* Level 5 Core Words—heavy stock, one per student to use as a reference for correcting their tests. It's in the back of the Sourcebook. By the way, if parents want a copy, I give it to them. This is the list of words from which the test words are taken throughout the year.
* Take-Home Tasks for the first few units, one for every student. These are homework blackline masters found inside each unit.
* Unit tests, one for each student, found inside each unit. For my grade level, there are two blackline masters—one testing words and one evaluating skills and proofreading/editing ability.
* Personal Posters, the five blackline masters introduced with the big Teaching Posters. They are in the back of the Sourcebook.

- I have my students make their Spelling Notebook (construction paper cover for about six blank sheets of lined paper). Students record words they miss on the unit tests in this notebook. It provides a record of missed words, about three   columns to a page, for study and reference.

Prepare the Spelling Notebooks.

- I start a file folder for each child in which I keep their Priority Word papers. Last year I also kept their unit tests in the folder, but this year parents want me to send the tests home.

Prepare file folders.

- I begin informally scrutinizing my students' writing, noting the words they miss most often. This provides information I'll need later when I start the Priority Words. I begin this part of the program about a month after I begin the first unit.

Prepare for Priority Words.

To begin, I open my Sourcebook to Unit 1—no prior review is necessary. On the first page of every unit is a headline: Build Skills and Word Experiences. It is the first main part of every unit. Here, I've learned that my teaching focus is exactly what that header says—skills and word experiences. It's similar to the way I teach reading: the foremost goal is to get kids comfortable *reading*, which means teaching them a lot of different skills, rather than just providing practice on a specific list of words. Likewise, in the Sourcebook program, the goal is to get kids comfortable *spelling in writing*, which means teaching them a lot of different skills, rather than just providing practice on a specific list of words. Teaching specific words, the Spelling Words, comes later in the second main part of every unit, Assess Words and Skills.

Instruction begins with skills and word experiences instead of a word list—just like the focus for teaching reading.

I do the first activity on the first page of the unit, the Word Preview in the Build Visual Skills section. It takes five minutes. Under the Word Preview logo, as with all logos, there is a page reference for the Teaching Notes that tell how to do the procedure. This explanatory information was essential for me at first and saved me time. For example, I learned that the procedure can be given any day of the week—overly obvious I suppose, but not to a beginner who still had an old mind-set for teaching spelling Monday-Friday.

The Word Preview opens a unit with a quick visual warm-up.

The Preview also confused some of my colleagues before their "new way" of thinking clicked in. They thought its purpose was to pretest the spelling words—not so! The words used for the Word Preview *are not the spelling words*—they are not posted in the classroom; they are not sent home. The words on the Preview are the Core Words used in each unit to "grow" or "drive" the skill-building lessons.

At first, I didn't use the Exercise Express, the next set of activities in every unit. They're optional, so I never explored them. Now I use them for extra credit—at home or at school. There's a generic blackline master for each one, which I prepare for my "centers." Some of the activities are quite challenging, while others are easy—all reinforce language skills. I probably should do more with Exercise Express, because the other fifth grade teachers say this is their students' favorite part!

The Exercise Express is a menu of optional spelling and language-related skills.

In the next section of each unit, I reuse the Core Words to explore more skills. It is called Build Basic Concepts—the section with the Seeds for Sowing Skills logo.   I somewhat randomly select what I want to teach—that's why I think it's called "sowing skills." I don't use a fixed routine, yet it's not an aimless approach either. There is a menu of skill-building activities, so I just choose the ones in each unit that seem right—the right difficulty, fit into my time frame, and are activities the kids need. The more I work with the program, the easier it is for me to select activities.

The teacher selects appropriate skill-building activities in Seeds for Sowing Skills.

Now I *differentiate* practice—all students are on the same concept, but I tailor the program so some students do more difficult activities, while others do easier ones. The best way to challenge my spelling "whiz kids" is through thought-provoking activities in which they are challenged to think about words, rules, exceptions, etymologies, and all the elements that make up our language. Likewise, the best route for keeping my lower performers on task is having them do activities that they *can* do and that benefit them.

Differentiated instruction is encouraged.

The instructional format I choose for an activity often determines its difficulty. For example, my capable students may be successful completing an activity as homework, while my less-able students will be successful with the same lesson only if I direct it.

Activity formats vary with teacher discretion.

I'm free to select the activities, as well as the formats, to customize the lessons to my students' needs. For example, in Activity 1A of Unit 8, I chose one of my most capable students to demonstrate how the *ly* suffix is added to words ending in consonant-*y*, such as *happy* and *busy*. Then I divided my class into small groups to find and write more words that behave the same way. Each group had a leader that recorded the words, but I was the recorder for a group of lower-performing students so that I could provide direction. Then we made a cumulative list of these words on a chart (e.g., *heavily, easily, luckily*) and I asked students to be on the lookout for more words that followed this spelling pattern. For some less-able students, their homework assignment that night was to find more of these words.

The next part of the 1A lesson was assigned for homework for my able learners that evening. They were asked to explore how to add the *able* suffix to these words: *measure, notice,* and *change*; and to write the rules that describe the actions. The next day, these students led the discussion that started the collection of words for two more charts—words that drop the final *e* before the addition of *able* (e.g., *measurable*) and words that end in *ce* or *ge* that do not drop the final *e* (e.g., *noticeable, changeable*). Students were to gather words over time to add to the charts. They would write the words on post-it notes and stick them to the chart, later to be added to the chart by me.

Students learn to be discriminating observers of words through multiple opportunities to collect and analyze words.

Activity 1A has several parts, and the last part students did independently in class. To begin, I wrote *thermos, miss, dash, beach, fox,* and *buzz* on the chalkboard, and students were to add the *s/es* suffix. We concluded that words ending in *s, ss, sh, ch, x,* and *z* add *es*, not *s*. Then students were to find and write more words to illustrate this rule. My two most capable students were assigned the task of identifying the *o*-ending words that also add *es* instead of just *s* (e.g., *potatoes*). At the end of the day, students turned to a partner to share their words and to proofread their work before handing it in, and the *o*-ending words were presented to the class by the students who had worked on that project.

I can't begin to do all the activities, and don't even try to do them all, because I've learned that when I skip them, they resurface in a slightly different way in subsequent units. The program recycles skills and concepts, but on occasion, I resurrect activities that I initially bypassed.

Skills and concepts are recycled.

I use Build Skillful Writers, the next section in each unit, mainly for my capable students to refine their writing. The lesson in Unit 13 on uncluttering writing by eliminating "double trouble" phrases made a big impact! My proficient writers still collect examples that meet this criterion (*end result, free gift, unexpected surprise*).

Sometimes we all get involved in Build Skillful Writers, such as the lesson on capital letters in Unit 21, or in Unit 22 when we focused on overused words in writing. I like how this section bonds spelling and writing.

As I said, I'm not an expert, but whatever I'm doing is working, because the kids enjoy it and they're learning. They see the reading and writing connections, their vocabularies are expanding through the word etymology features, they have truly become interested in words—they collect words, examine words, sort words, discuss words, use words, spell words. The number of words to which they are exposed is far more than in my old word-list programs. This is not just a spelling program— I use my Sourcebook as a source to expand and balance my total Language Communications instruction.

The next section is not one I take casually. It's called Build Assessment Readiness next to the Test Ready logo. Here I ready my class on the skill that's tested later in the unit—the skill is noted in the margin. There's a school lesson and a homework lesson. Because some of my students rarely get much help at home, I often have them do the homework Take-Home Task at school. It's on a blackline master in each unit. For parents who can participate, the Take-Home Task brings them into the skill-building loop with their child.

Proofreading is the next section in each unit, but I don't see it as something I *do* next—it's ongoing in students' everyday writing. The skill-building lessons teach students how to spell and proofread. Then they apply their skills in writing. I relinquish the role of being their personal editor for an increasing number of words over time as they develop as writers. These words that I now expect them to religiously proofread are their Priority Words. I expect my students to proofread with 100% accuracy as they use them across the curriculum in their everyday writing. Everyday writing includes all writing with the exception of writing-as-a-process papers for which 100% accuracy is expected for all words.

I start my class on Priority Words in October—I follow the suggestions in the Teaching Notes. Until then, I get my feet on the ground with the regular activities, and I look at my students' writing to determine the initial Priority Word expectation. Many students confuse the "*there*" homophones, so we usually start with words 1–36 on a frequency-of-use list, just short of #37, which is *there*.

I never put a word on the Priority Word list that I anticipate my students will miss in their writing. This year I gave my students six weeks to prepare for the addition of *there* and its partners, *their* and *they're*, that are added at the same time. Students who needed help were identified, not only through their writing, but also on the Cloze Story Word Tests that always include these homophones.

Each student has a Spell Check® card, an alphabetical list of the top 150 high-use writing words, on which I signal the current Priority Words with a yellow highlighter. Last year I didn't have the Spell Check® cards, so I used the Priority Words blackline master to signal the Priority Words. Most students have exactly the same words highlighted, but this year I have two students with fewer words and three students with more. So most students started with 36 words highlighted, and by the end of the year I anticipate we'll progress up the frequency-of-use list to a total of 100. It's an ongoing process of adding words. Most words are not as challenging as *there/their/they're*, so I can add them with little fanfare, sometimes adding two or three sequential words at one time, as students become more capable.

Spelling is for "using" words in writing at all levels, but becomes a regular unit section beginning in Level 4.

The Sourcebooks provide a resource for a balanced Language Communications program—the books are more than spelling.

Skills are taught and tested.

Students are taught how to spell and proofread, and then they are expected to apply their skills in writing.

Priority Words are the highest-frequency words in writing and are the words most often carelessly misspelled or misused in writing.

A highlighting marker can signal the Priority Words on each student's Spell Check card or on the Priority Word blackline master.

I'm genuinely surprised how easily my students learn words that were always the source of errors on our district writing tests, as well as in their everyday writing. These words include demons such as *because*, *until*, *they*, and the "*there*," "*your*," and "*its*" homophones. I always provide proofreading time before papers are handed in, and my students are not threatened by this, but work together with their references to proofread. The level of student effort and the sincere pride my students take in a well-proofread paper truly amazes me. Students develop the habit of proofreading their Priority Words, which teaches them the skills necessary for proofreading *any word*, as well as for performing well on standardized spelling tests—all of which are editing tests. It works!

Students develop a proof-reading habit and take pride in their work.

Priority Words are the *minimum expectation* for spelling accuracy in everyday writing. Sometimes I complement this set of words with a dozen or so Special Words, also called Topical Words, students need for writing on a particular topic. These words are treated as Priority Words for that one assignment or unit of study. Spelling Priority Words and Special Words correctly is something I expect—and I inspect.

Expectations require inspections.

I evaluate about eight or nine randomly selected papers for every student during a grading period, usually one a week. I thought this would be time consuming, but I use Rebecca Sitton's method of bracketing a section of a paper for inspection, and it's quick. At first I was afraid I'd fail to spot a Priority Word error when I checked papers. I didn't know the words by heart. So I used a suggestion I learned in the training seminar. I told students that if they found an error I failed to find, it counted against ME, not them. They love looking for my errors!

Marking papers for Priority Words is quick.

Once papers are checked, I write the names of students for whom I've checked a paper on the chalkboard and put their papers in a basket. Students look at their papers, fix errors if necessary, return their papers to the basket before the end of the day, and erase their name from the chalkboard. I file the papers in a folder for each student. The papers do not have a grade, but I've noted whether the student met the expectation—and they usually do, for it's highly unusual for a student to miss these words on which we have placed such importance. A powerful follow-up includes a friendly handshake to celebrate each student's continued effort and achievement of this expectation!

Students receive feedback and positive reinforcement.

At my school, students' ability to spell the "no excuses" words definitely figures into their grade. For students to qualify for an A on the report card for spelling, they must have a clean record for Priority Words and any added Special Words. Even if they don't get an A because of the other things that figure into the grade, I write on their report card that they spelled their Priority Words correctly in their writing. Priority Words are a big thing in our classroom—and in our school.

The ability to spell Priority Words in everyday writing figures into students' grades.

Next, I begin the second main part of every unit—Assess Words and Skills. It is announced with the same headline as the first part, Build Skills and Word Experiences. Now my focus changes to evaluation. First, I evaluate students' ability to spell the essential words necessary for everyday writing. This makes sense; otherwise, how would I know which words they need to study?

Evaluation is the focus in Assess Words and Skills.

The first activity is the Cloze Story Word Test on which all previously introduced Core Words in the program—all the way back to word #1, *the*—are evaluated. Students do not study the test words prior to the test, so that I can assess long-term, not short-term, mastery of words. I make copies of the blackline master Word Test and give each student a copy—nothing else is on their desk. I read the whole story aloud while my students follow the words with their eyes. Then they write their name on their test. Next, I read just enough of the story to include the first blank, and then I ask my class what word goes in that blank—they shout it out,

The Cloze Story Word Test assesses long-term mastery of all previously introduced Core Words in the program.

then write it. In my class, they print, which probably isn't necessary but I don't want them to argue with me about whether it's an *e* or an *i*, or whatever.

After the test, I correct it in the same way I did my old Friday Tests—I circle missed words. The words students miss are their Spelling Words. I record the grades (-4 if they missed four), and then with a copy of the Core Words Blackline Master for a reference, students write their Spelling Words three times: once correctly on their test paper, once on their Words to Learn sheet for take-home study, and once in their Spelling Notebook for their at-school record.

Spelling Words are identified for study.

I remind my students to study their Spelling Words at home or school in preparation for upcoming tests. It's fun to watch their surprise when the words resurface on subsequent Cloze Story Word Tests and their discovery that the end of a unit does not signal the end of their obligation for correctly spelling the words, as in their previous spelling programs. They're learning to be "forever spellers," not "Friday spellers."

Students learn to be "forever spellers," not "Friday spellers."

Now I have time-effectively identified words each student does not know, and I have targeted their study to these specific words, mastery of which is necessary to improve their writing. The easiest way to improve students' writing is the most obvious, and consequently the most often overlooked—improve their spelling. Students do not have predetermined, one-size-fits-all lists, but lists individualized to their spelling needs. And the program automatically retests all of these words for me on subsequent tests—over and over again. With no extra effort or recordkeeping on my part, the words are recycled, providing maximum practice to ensure mastery.

Spelling study is individualized, targeted to words each student needs to learn to be a better writer.

If the test is too hard for some students, I make it easier by filling in a few blanks on the test with a yellow highlighter—they trace over these words. If the test is too easy for some students, I make it more challenging by also giving them the optional Sentence Dictation Test. I also identify missed words in their writing for them to record in the More Words for Super Spellers section of their Words to Learn sheet, and I ask them to add words they'd like to learn to spell.

Testing can be differentiated.

There is another testing master that I do the next day or so—it contains the Skill Test, which tests the skill presented in Build Assessment Readiness, and the Proofreading Test (grades 5–8), which prepares students for standardized spelling tests. (I understand the Skill Test is on the same blackline master as the Cloze Story Word Test in grades 1–4.) I never skip the Proofreading Test, not only because of its proofing practice, but it teaches the importance of reading and following directions, and it prepares my students for standardized spelling tests. Our seventh and eighth grade teachers love the content of the Proofreading Tests—a chronology of American History—because spelling is taught in their English/Social Studies classes.

Grading is now more credible, because there are several indicators of spelling growth. As a school, we discussed how to grade spelling and decided on these guidelines, which we shared with parents and students. The final spelling grade for each quarter acknowledges students' performance mainly on—

Students' spelling grades can depend upon several areas of growth.

- spelling Priority Words and any Special Words correctly in writing, judged from randomly selected writing samples across the curriculum—about one a week per student in grades 1–6, and two or three samples for grades 7–8.
- word tests—the Cloze Story Word Test and, for some students, the Sentence Dictation Test.

Further, we decided to consider these indicators as well—

- spelling skill-building assignments, judged from randomly selected assignments—perhaps about ten per student.
- other tests—the Skill Test and the Proofreading Test.

- spelling in the writing process, judged from students' ability to complete the assignment as indicated with a 100% standard for spelling all words accurately.

This information is gathered and recorded throughout the grading period. Students are informed every step of the way. Students who hand in their assignments, do well on their tests, and meet the minimum expectation for spelling in everyday writing through accuracy on their Priority Words can count on a good spelling grade.

The Teaching Notes in the back of the Sourcebooks include a long list of ideas to keep parents in the spelling "loop." Some parents asked me to send home the Cloze Story Word Tests, so I do for all students; I provide the list of Level 5 Core Words, if requested; I usually send home Take-Home Tasks; I always send the Words to Learn list home with Ideas for Word Study copied on the back; and I send packets of papers for proofreading that I have purposely not marked for Priority Words, accompanied by a copy of the Ideas for Proofreading Blackline Master which offers suggestions to parents to help their child proofread. On the back of this master, I copy the Priority Words Blackline Master on which students circle their current words.

Opportunities for parents to participate are abundant.

Every unit is laid out the same way, actually very structured. However, my instruction varies, so the time frame for a unit varies, and that is my choice. For example, sometimes I do more activities, and on occasion I may do the Sentence Dictation for the whole class as a proofreading activity by providing the sentences for checking. With this freedom, I'm a better teacher and it's easier for me to teach.

Each unit follows the same framework, but the instruction can vary.

Next year, the sixth grade teachers will begin on the first unit of their Sourcebooks regardless of where each fifth grade class ended. The same goes for all grade levels. Skills are revisited and Core Words that students did not have experiences with or do not know how to spell will surface on subsequent Cloze Story Word Tests that test all previously introduced words. It is a spiraling system that works.

Skills and words spiral level to level.

I'm in my twenty-fourth year of teaching, and before using the Sourcebook Series   I never felt I was truly teaching my kids to spell. Spelling was a word list. Now spelling is for writing. The paradigm change necessary for success with this program evolved for all of us. The other day at our faculty meeting, we recalled the stress we felt early on and laughed—How did the Friday Test ever help kids, anyway?

Spelling is for writing.

I'm looking forward to teaching another year. This year we'll use the Student Practice Books for Learning Spelling and Word Skills. We used them in our summer curriculum and they were a big success for low and high achievers! They make skill teaching more focused—and easier! So, we're all set to engage kids in language learning via the Sourcebooks and Practice Books this year!

The Student Practice Books engage students of all ability levels.

Apples, Apples Everywhere

For forty-nine years, Johnny Appleseed sprinkled bucketfuls of apple seeds across the countryside of hills and valleys. It has been said of this man, whose real name was John Chapman, that he dreamed of apples, apples everywhere for every one of us to share!

Your Core Words, like the seeds within the core of an apple, help you create a recipe for teaching spelling— you're the chef! You can prepare a "lighter fare" meal for your classroom, or a "hearty" meal that serves up all the side dishes, too.

To add to your cookbook, I offer you one of my best recipes—a no-fail pie crust for a traditional apple pie! No matter what I create in the kitchen, friends and family seem to like "old favorites" best. So, for cooking and for teaching, I respect the basics. Nothing is more basic than a return to the skills, concepts, and expectations that are clearly the centerpiece of my spelling methodology; and nothing can displace good, old-fashioned apple pie! Enjoy!

You-Deserve-It Apple Pie

I don't usually measure precisely—nor will you need to. You can't go wrong with this old-fashioned, best-loved dessert.

No-Fail Pie Crust

I searched for the best pie crust recipe. I've used this one for years, having found it written on a scrap of paper inside an old-time cookbook in a used bookstore. It was labeled Florence's No-Fail Pie Crust—my thanks to Florence.

First, make sure everything is cold—I even refrigerate my bowl before beginning. Of course, I live in the Scottsdale desert.

Combine in a bowl—
1. 3 cups all-purpose flour
2. 1 t salt
3. 1 3/4 cups shortening (regular Crisco)

Cut in shortening with a pastry cutter until pieces are about marble-sized, or so.

Add—
4. 6 T ice water
5. 2 T of something acidic, such as white vinegar or orange juice
6. 1 jumbo egg, or two small ones

Mix until it's a gooey ball. Separate into two parts—one amount slightly more than the other.

Place a handful of flour on a cold pastry cloth. Place the larger amount of dough on top of the flour. Roll out to about 1/8 inch thickness—I always use a roller sleeve on my roller. Then roll the dough onto the roller, lift, and place in the center of the pie plate. Tuck down. Don't worry if pastry tears—just patch and mend—it won't show.

Apple Filling

Peel and cut into equally thin wedges—
7. 6–8 apples—Golden Delicious are excellent

Add and mix—
8. 1 C all-purpose flour
9. 1 C white sugar
10. 1/2 C brown sugar, or a little more
11. dashes of cinnamon, nutmeg, allspice
12. sometimes I add a little vanilla

Pour apples into pastry crust in pie plate. Make a mountain of apples.

Dot on—
13. a few slices of butter—go for it!

Roll out the remaining dough for the top crust, as before, and add to top of the pie. Trim the overlapping pastry. Seal the top and bottom crust edges and press to the rim of the pie plate.

Beat until foamy—
14. 1 egg
Spread egg foam over pastry, mending the pastry, as needed. Cut slices in the pastry for steam to escape—it's fun to cut the initials of a family member or guest.

Top with a generous sprinkle of raw sugar—your store will have it—
15. raw sugar

Bake at 400 degrees for about 15 minutes. Reduce to 350 degrees until crust is golden—about 30–40 minutes.

Enjoy! Rebecca

 By the way, if you have extra dough, here's a real treat! Roll out the pastry and cut it into pieces about 3 inches square. Put on a dab of jam, a slice of butter, seal, place on a cookie sheet, and cook. These are for the kids (and you!) to eat immediately after they're baked. Save the pie for dessert. I call these pie rolls and I like them best of all!

Build Skills and Word Experiences

Use Student Practice Pages 49–50 to follow up instruction for:
Activity 1A • Activities 3A, 3B

all students participate

Build Visual Skills

Do the Word Preview, a visual warm-up activity, with all students.
Use Core Words **sure** (251), **knew** (252), **it's** (253), **try** (254), **told** (255).

Teaching Notes, page 331

totally optional, can use if you want to

Build Spelling and Language Skills

Choose from among these quick tasks to customize instruction
for all or selected students.

Teaching Notes, page 334

  It's across the way.

  What was that sound. Father tolld the children to try there best to keep very still. Soon they all new for shure that it was only the water.
(question mark, *told*, *their*, *knew*, *sure*)

  knew, right, sure, come, light, know, large, high, have
(e.g., silent letter *k/gh/e*; number of letters)

  my, try, by, why, _____, _____, _____, _____
(words that end in long *i* spelled *y*)

  It's always hard for me to tell my mother _____.

  Words that show possession, or ownership
(e.g., Mary's, theirs, its)

161

Teaching Notes, page 339

contractions, writing words,
class book

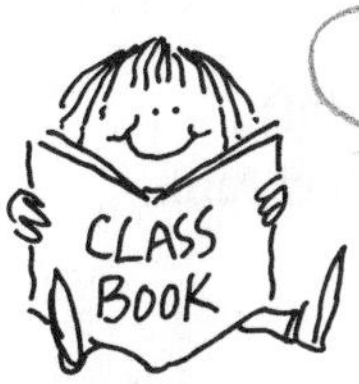

Build Basic Concepts

Choose from among these skill-building activities to customize instruction
for all or selected students.

| concept one | A contraction is a combination of two or more words with an apostrophe replacing a letter or letters. |

1A Organize students into six cooperative groups. Assign a contraction set to each: *will/shall*, *would/had*, *have*, *is/has*, *not*, *are*. Have groups brainstorm contractions. Then discuss the results of each group's effort. Make a complete list of contractions on the chalkboard. Include *I'm* and *let's*. Next, use the *not* and *are* contractions for review (Activity 3A, page 34) and the others to further your class book series on contractions.

have
I've
you've
we've
they've
what've
who've

not
can't
don't
isn't
won't
shouldn't
couldn't
wouldn't
aren't
doesn't
wasn't
weren't
hasn't
haven't
hadn't
mustn't
didn't
mightn't
oughtn't
needn't

is/has
he's
she's
it's
what's
that's
who's
there's
here's
where's

will/shall
I'll
you'll
she'll
he'll
it'll
we'll
they'll
who'll
what'll

would/had
I'd
you'd
he'd
she'd
we'd
they'd
who'd

are
you're
we're
they're
who're
what're

word analysis, homophones,
writing sentences, contractions,
possessive pronouns

1B Demonstrate testing *its/it's* for which is correct: If it makes sense to say *it is*, use *it's*. If not, use *its*. Dictate these sentences for students to write. After each, write the sentence on the chalkboard and apply the test.

It's time to go.   The dog is in its house.
The animal ate its food.   Its picture is in the paper.
Tell us when it's over.   We all think it's great.

Follow up with students writing sentences for *it's* and *its*. Then have students read their sentences to a partner. The partner responds with the correct *it's/its*.

Have students make word cards (use the Word Card Blackline Master, page 401) for *it's/its*. Say sentences that use *it's/its* and have students hold up the correct card. Reuse these cards as needed.

1C Demonstrate testing *lets/let's* for which is correct: If it makes sense to say *let us*, use *let's*. If not, use *lets*. Dictate these sentences for students to write. After each sentence, write the sentence on the chalkboard and apply the test.

word analysis, writing sentences, contractions, homophones

Let's play ball!	She lets her hair dry in the sun.
He lets me in for free.	He said, "Let's be quiet."
Let's go home.	Who lets the dog out at night?

Follow up with students writing sentences for *let's* and *lets*. Then have students read their sentences to a partner. The partner responds with the correct *let's/lets*.

Have students make word cards (use the WORD CARD BLACKLINE MASTER, page 401) for *let's/lets*. Say sentences that use *let's/lets* and have students hold up the correct card. Reuse these cards as needed.

example

1D Post Teaching Poster 1. Chant the rhyme and review *there/their/they're*. Then ask students to write the contraction *they're* in its longer form (they are). Next, ask students to find a sentence in print material that uses *they're*. Have them write the sentence—then rewrite it using *they are*.

homophones, contractions, writing sentences

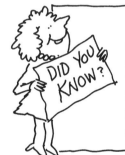

DID YOU KNOW?

Many people are very busy, so shortcuts that save time and effort are widespread. A speech and writing time-saver is the contraction. Shortcuts, such as *don't* and *can't*, began circa 1642. Yet, the use of contractions was forbidden in formal writing because it was thought to reflect sloppy speech. This prohibition is now eroding, however, and contractions are no longer considered careless or too casual for most written work.

no connection between concept 1 & concept 2

concept two	Some words have silent letters.

2A Write on the chalkboard: *rose, write, line, above, sure*. Ask students how these words are alike (final silent *e*). Remind students that some words have silent letters. Review final silent *e* words using student-made word cards (Activity 1A, page 102). Then, working in pairs, one student draws a word card from the pile (face down) and gives a clue for the word. The partner writes the word. Then the spelling is checked against the word card. Redistribute the word cards and have students replay the game.

phonics, word analysis, spelling game

2B Select a student to write *knew* on the chalkboard. Underline the silent *k*. Provide clues for students to identify more silent *k* words (e.g., knife, knee, know, knit, kneel, knock, knuckle, knead). Write the words on the chalkboard as students predict the spelling. Then have students gather knock-knock jokes from among those they've heard or those in joke books (e.g., Knock. Knock. Who's there? Lettuce. Lettuce who? Lettuce in, and you'll find out!). Create a class book of knock-knock jokes.

phonics, more words, predicting spelling, creating a book

163

phonics, writing names

2C Ask students to take turns writing their name on the chalkboard. Then identify the silent letters in students' names.

phonics, writing words, more words, game

2D Revisit the silent *k* words (Activity 2B, this unit). Review silent *t* and *w*, as in *often* and *write* (Activity 2A, page 34); and *gh* and *mb*, as in *high* and *lamb* (Activity 1D, page 102). Make a generous list of words with silent letters on the chalkboard. Then have student pairs select a word to begin a word chain to add to the word chain bulletin board (Activity 1A, page 152).

concept three	A prefix is a letter or letters added to the beginning of a word. A suffix is a letter or letters added to the end of a word.

prefix practice, suffix practice, vocabulary development, more words, predicting spelling, writing sentences, art

3A Write on the chalkboard: *He's sure that it's his bike.* Then challenge students to change *sure* to *not sure* in the sentence by writing only two letters (*unsure*). Have a student change *sure* to *unsure* in the sentence. Remind students that a prefix is a letter or letters added to the beginning of a word—*un* is a prefix. Have students brainstorm more words with the *un* prefix (e.g., unable, uneven, unused, unwritten, unwanted, unkind, unhappy, unclean, undo, unlucky). Write the words on the chalkboard as students predict the spelling. Help students discover that the *un* prefix means not or opposite of.

Note that prefixes change the meaning of a word. Suffixes generally do not change the meaning of a word, but change its use by changing the part of speech.

Ask students what we call a letter or letters added to the end of a word (suffix). Write *surely* on the chalkboard. Use *surely* in oral sentences to confirm its meaning. Note that the final silent *e* is not dropped because the suffix doesn't begin with a vowel. This principle is usually true; however, one exception is *true* (*truly*). Have students find and write more words that end in silent *e* to which the *ly* suffix can be added (e.g., lonely, completely, lively).

Have students fold story paper in half to make two boxes. In one box have them write and illustrate a sentence using a word with the *un* prefix. In the other, have them write and illustrate the same sentence, but with the *un* prefix removed from the word (e.g., It is unnecessary to call me. It is necessary to call me.). This activity helps students contrast the meaning of words with/without the *un* prefix.

DID YOU KNOW?

The most common spelling of /sh/ is *ti*, as in *nation*. This accounts for about 53% of the /sh/ spellings. Of course, *sh* spells this sound—26% of the time. Words with a French origin spell the sound with *ch*, for example *chic* and *chef*. Other /sh/ spellings include *ci* (special), *ce* (ocean), *ss* (pressure), *si* (mission), and *sci* (conscious). The /sh/ is spelled with a single *s* in only two words (or their word forms)—*sugar* and *sure*.

• Challenge students to find words in which the initial *s* spells /sh/.

3B Write on the chalkboard: *Please tell the story again.* Read the sentence—then cross out *again*. Ask students to add a prefix to a word in the sentence that will make the sentence mean exactly the same thing (retell). Ask students what we call letters added to the beginning of a word (prefix—*re* is a prefix). Have students work in pairs to brainstorm more words with the *re* prefix (e.g., relive, replace, rewrite, reopen, remodel, restudy, replay, replant, reread, reorder, redo, reuse, refill). Award students one point for each accurate word. Make a cumulative list on the chalkboard. Note that *re* means again or back. Then have students write the words in alphabetical order.

prefix practice, writing words, more words, alphabetizing, vocabulary development

3C Post Teaching Poster 3. Write *tell* on the chalkboard. Have students write *tell* and suffix forms of *tell* (tells, telling, told, teller). Write the words on the chalkboard for students to self-check. Note that the *ed* suffix is not added to *tell*—instead the spelling is changed to *told* in the past tense. Provide practice with more irregular verbs by dictating these verbs for students to write their irregular past tense forms: *make, have, find, write, think, come, give, keep, know.* Then write the words on the chalkboard for students to self-check.

suffix practice, other word forms, writing words, irregular verbs, proofreading

a basic component

Build Assessment Readiness

Use these at-school and at-home exercises to prepare all students for the Skill Test.

Teaching Notes, page 343

at-school Ask students to write contractions. Time the session (about three minutes). Have students take turns writing one of their contractions on the chalkboard. Then choose another student to write its longer form next to it.

Skill to be tested: contractions

at-home Send home a copy of TAKE-HOME TASK 17 BLACKLINE MASTER, page 166, with each student to encourage parent-child partnerships.

Skill to be tested: contractions

Build Proofreading Skills

Provide spelling application opportunities for all students.

Teaching Notes, page 344

don't use at beginning of term so that spelling

Track students' ability to meet a minimum competency for spelling and proofreading within selected samples of their everyday writing.

• Send home papers for proofreading and, if necessary, a copy of the IDEAS FOR PROOFREADING BLACKLINE MASTER, page 390.

> Students get more spelling practice than ever as they proofread for Priority Words in their everyday writing assignments across the curriculum.

165

Name _____

Dear Parents,

Finish this jingle with your child. Then gather the family and read the rhyme chorally. Clap it, stamp it, and enjoy it! Try substituting your names in the rhyme. It's fun!

Shortcuts

If I will not, I say I _____!

If I do not, I say I _____!

If I could not, I say I _____!

If I should not, I say I _____!

It works the same for would and _____!

that is _____   you are _____

they are _____   I will _____

you have _____   we have _____

there is _____   cannot _____

do not _____   it is _____

what is _____   we are _____

Continue to practice contractions with your child by making more "shortcut" words. We're working on contractions at school, too—but your help at home is excellent practice for your child. Thank you!

Sourcebook 3, Unit 17

127

Assess Words and Skills

- Spelling Words (words missed on tests) are recorded in the Spelling Notebook.
- Use Proof It, Practice Page 51, for proofreading/editing practice.

WORD TEST

Teaching Notes, page 350

Assess Spelling Progress

Give this Cloze Story Word Test of Core Words within the frequencies 1–255 to all students. Words students miss are their Spelling Words.

BEFORE THE CLOZE STORY WORD TEST

Students do not prestudy the words. Provide students with a copy of REVIEW 17 BLACKLINE MASTER, page 170. Tell students that this story will have them singing.

THE CLOZE STORY WORD TEST

Read the entire story aloud, including the test words. Then read it again slowly as students write the missing words.

WORD TEST

Sing a Song

(1) <u>There</u> is a song you (2) <u>knew</u> when you were (3) <u>little</u>. You (4) <u>still</u> sing it (5) <u>today</u>. It is (6) <u>sure</u> to be sung to you (7) <u>once</u> a year. We are (8) <u>told</u> that (9) <u>it's</u> the most (10) <u>often</u> sung song! Mildred Hill, a Kentucky (11) <u>school</u> teacher, wrote the melody, and her sister, Patty Hill, a principal, wrote (12) <u>its</u> words. (13) <u>However</u>, long ago the words were (14) <u>different</u>. The song (15) <u>began</u>, "Good morning to all, Good morning to all." (16) <u>Try</u> to sing this song with these words. (17) <u>Then</u> write the song the way all of us (18) <u>know</u> it best.

Words tested:
there (37), then (53), its (76), little (92), know (100), different (139), still (153), often (186), school (194), once (206), began (215), today (249), however, (250), sure (251), knew (252), it's (253), try (254), told (255)

AFTER THE CLOZE STORY WORD TEST

1. Have students recall and write the words to the familiar song, "Happy Birthday." Then write the words on the chalkboard for students to self-check. Discuss the meaning of melody. Follow up by challenging students to write the words to one of their favorite songs.

writing, proofreading

2. Have students record the words they missed on the test
   - in their Spelling Notebook (see page 353) for at-school study, and
   - on a copy of the WORDS TO LEARN BLACKLINE MASTER, page 392, for at-home study.

Send home the completed WORDS TO LEARN personal study list and, if necessary, a copy of the IDEAS FOR WORD STUDY BLACKLINE MASTER, page 391.

recording words for personal study list

CLOZE STORY SKILL-BUILDING EXTENSIONS

visual skill building, writing an explanation, contractions

1. Have students circle and write the story words *it's* and *its*. Have them explain in writing how these words are used differently.

visual skill building, multiple meanings, writing sentences

2. Have students circle and write the story words *still*, *long*, and *way*. Then have students write each word in two sentences, each sentence using a different meaning for the word. Have students share their sentences.

visual skill building, writing words, alphabetizing

3. Have students find and circle the story words *when*, *were*, *wrote*, *words*, *with*, and *way*. Then have students write the words in alphabetical order.

suffix practice, more words, writing words, irregular verbs

4. Have students write the story words *sing*, *write*, and *know*. Then have them add the appropriate suffixes and write the past tense word forms. Next, have students find and write more base words for which *ed* cannot be added, but the spelling changes instead.

compound words, writing words

5. Have students write the compound word *birthday*. Then have students find and write more compound words.

Assess Skill Application

Give this assessment of spelling and related skills to all students.

Teaching Notes, page 354

BEFORE THE SKILL TEST

Direct students' attention to the Skill Test at the bottom of REVIEW 17 BLACKLINE MASTER, page 170. Read the directions as students follow along.

THE SKILL TEST

Skill tested: contractions

Make contractions.

it	is	that	there	not	can	do
are	will	us	let	we	who	you

it's, that's, there's, who's, we're, who're, you're, we'll,

who'll, it'll, you'll, won't, isn't, aren't, can't, don't, let's

AFTER THE SKILL TEST

Note the ability of each student to write contractions. Use the Word Test to evaluate each student's ability to discriminate between *it's/its*.

Sourcebook 3, Unit 17

129

alternative for kids needing challenge

SENTENCE DICTATION

Teaching Notes, page 355

Extend Spelling Assessment

Give this in-context assessment of Core Words within the frequencies 1–255 to students who need more practice or challenge.

 BEFORE THE SENTENCE DICTATION TEST

Students do not prestudy the words. Provide students with writing paper and pencil.

 THE SENTENCE DICTATION TEST

Have students write the sentences as they are dictated.

SENTENCE DICTATION

1. The school play and music show will begin soon.

2. It's sure to be an important night on the stage.

3. The children were told by everyone to try very hard.

4. Their mothers and fathers knew they wanted to do their best.

Words tested:
the (1), and (3), to (5), on (14), they (19), be (21), by (27), were (34), an (39), their (42), do (45), will (46), very (93), show (184), want(ed) (193), school (194), important (195), children (200), mother(s) (226), father(s) (229), night (231), soon (236), hard (242), best (246), sure (251), knew (252), it's (253), try (254), told (255)

Extra words (see page 356): begin, everyone, music, play, stage

 AFTER THE SENTENCE DICTATION TEST

1. Based on what the sentences say, have students write how they think the children in the school play and music show are feeling. Have students write about a time they felt the same way. Remind students that their explanation should have a beginning, a middle, and an end.

speculating, writing

2. Have students record the words they missed on the test

• in their Spelling Notebook (see page 358) for at-school study, and

• on a copy of the WORDS TO LEARN BLACKLINE MASTER, page 392, for at-home study.

Send home the completed WORDS TO LEARN personal study list and, if necessary, a copy of the IDEAS FOR WORD STUDY BLACKLINE MASTER, page 391.

recording words for personal study list

THE CLOZE STORY WORD TESTS AND SENTENCE DICTATION TESTS ALLOW YOU, THE TEACHER, TO BE A BETTER PRACTITIONER. THESE TESTS IDENTIFY STUDENTS' SPELLING NEEDS. HOW CAN WE MEET STUDENTS' NEEDS WITHOUT KNOWING WHAT THEY ARE?

169

Word Test

Sing a Song

(1) _____ is a song you (2) _____ when you were

(3) _____. You (4) _____ sing it (5) _____. It

is (6) _____ to be sung to you (7) _____ a year. We are

(8) _____ that (9) _____ the most (10) _____

sung song! Mildred Hill, a Kentucky (11) _____ teacher, wrote the

melody, and her sister, Patty Hill, a principal, wrote (12) _____

words. (13) _____, long ago the words were (14) _____.

The song (15) _____, "Good morning to all, Good morning to all."

(16) _____ to sing this song with these words. (17) _____

write the song the way all of us (18) _____ it best.

Skill Test

Make contractions.

it	is	that	there	not	can	do
are	will	us	let	we	who	you

_____

_____

_____

A contraction is a shortcut word! The apostrophe takes the place of missing letters in contractions.

I am = I'm   let us = let's

Write contractions made from the words on the charts.

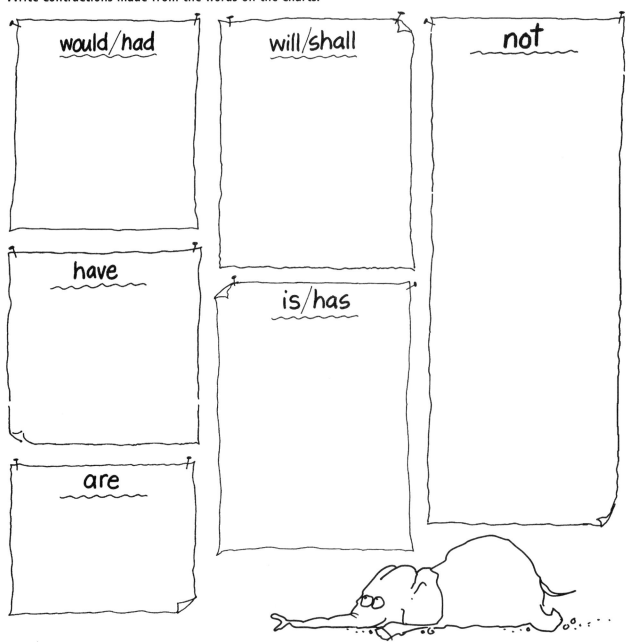

would/had

will/shall

not

have

is/has

are

Abbreviations are other shortcut words! Write the months of the year and the days of the week. Then, next to each one, write its abbreviation. How many other abbreviations can you find and write? Sort your abbreviations in some way.

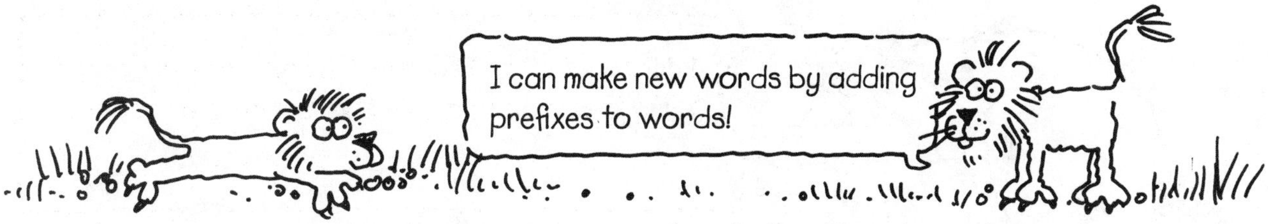

I can make new words by adding prefixes to words!

Add the re or un prefix to each word. Write the new word on the line. Then answer the question.

1. Add un to tied.

What might have happened when the zookeeper _____ the lion?

_____

2. Add un to usual.

What would be _____ weather for your city this time of year?

_____

3. Add re to use.

What items do you _____ at home instead of throwing them away?

_____

4. Add re to read.

Why might someone _____ a book?

_____

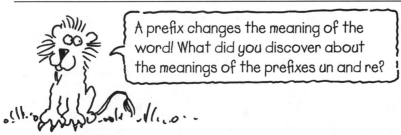

A prefix changes the meaning of the word! What did you discover about the meanings of the prefixes un and re?

1. When you add the un prefix, it changes the new word to mean

_____

2. When you add the re prefix, it changes the new word to mean

_____

Find and write more words that have the un and re prefixes. Are there words to which you might add either prefix—un or re—to make new words?

Circle one spelling error in each line. Then write the word right.

General Spaghetti is a special guy whoo lives in 1. ____________________

Spaghetti Land. Of course, this is won super spot 2. ____________________

to eat spaghetti, and you can be shure that the 3. ____________________

general stuffs himseff with the noodles and spicy 4. ____________________

sauce often. Yet, he stays vary busy with projects 5. ____________________

other than feasting on spaghetti. Once on a suny 6. ____________________

day, he had what he thuoght was an outstanding 7. ____________________

idea. They're were words that caused him a lot of 8. ____________________

spelling stress. So, he decided to hav a word sale 9. ____________________

to sell all the words that snarled his life. Soone 10. ____________________

it came to be. Buyers packed there sacks full of 11. ____________________

the troublesome words and carted then away! But 12. ____________________

then their were no words left—no words to read, to 13. ____________________

say, or to spell. What was the general too do now? 14. ____________________

on another paper

Read the story about General Spaghetti again. Count every "s" letter. Then answer this question: How many "s" letters are there in all?

Answer key for teachers indicates there are no s letters in the word all!

Build Skills and Word Experiences

UNIT 9

Use Student Practice Pages 25–26 to follow up instruction for:
Activity 1A • Test Ready

Build Visual Skills

Do the Word Preview, a visual warm-up activity, with all students.
Use Core Words **bright** (541), **sent** (542), **present** (543), **plan** (544), **rather** (545).

Teaching Notes, page 316

Build Spelling and Language Skills

Choose from among these quick tasks to customize instruction
for all or selected students.

Teaching Notes, page 319

 They sent a present.

 Our present plan is to paint the hallway with wild, bright color rather then brown or white. We have all ready send for the paint and will begin the moment it comes. Whose going to help us

(*colors*, *than*, *already*, *sent*, *Who's*, question mark)

 **rather, dollar, alligator, inventor, prettier, beaver, sailor, deeper, cougar, faster, jogger, rooster, beggar**

(e.g., ends in *ar/er/or*; vowel-*r* ending is part of base word/suffix meaning one who/suffix meaning more; does/doesn't contain double letters; is/isn't an animal word)

 bright, brighter, brightest; clear, clearer, clearest; _____

(words that are comparisons)

 One thing that I plan to do is _____

 Words that double the final letter before adding *ed* or *ing*

Have students write (**IN OTHER WORDS**): "Plan your day, then work your plan."
Norman Vincent Peale

73

Sourcebook 5, Unit 9

135

Teaching Notes, page 325

Build Basic Concepts

Choose from among these skill-building activities to customize instruction for all or selected students.

concept one	Some words are spelled with consonant digraphs.

phonics, word analysis, more words, sorting words, parts of speech

1A Select students to write on the chalkboard: *camp/champ, sort/short, ten/then, were/where, pony/phony*. Note that when *h* follows *c, s, t, w,* or *p* the combination stands for a new sound. Have students brainstorm words that contain each digraph at the beginning, middle, and end of the word. Help students discover that words do not end with *wh*.

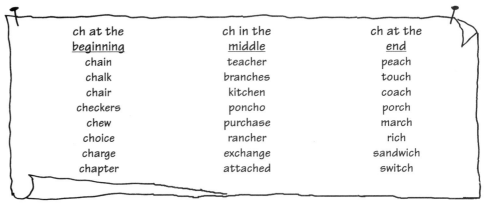

ch at the beginning	ch in the middle	ch at the end
chain	teacher	peach
chalk	branches	touch
chair	kitchen	coach
checkers	poncho	porch
chew	purchase	march
choice	rancher	rich
charge	exchange	sandwich
chapter	attached	switch

Challenge some students to sort the words by nouns, verbs, and words that can be both.

concept two	Some words are spelled with consonant blends.

phonics, writing word clues, reading

2A Review digraphs (Activity 1A) to point out that these adjacent consonants make one sound. But sometimes adjacent consonants make separate sounds that blend together. Write *present* on the chalkboard to point out how the separate sounds *pr* and *nt* are easier to spell when you listen to the sound of each of the letters. Have students write words with consonant blends, write clues for the words, and read the clues for their classmates to identify and write.

phonics, homographs, writing sentences, vocabulary development

2B Write on the chalkboard: *content, desert, object, present, record*. Have students identify the consonant blends (nt, rt, ct, pr, rd). Help students discover that these words can be pronounced in two ways, and each pronunciation has a different meaning. They are homographs (homographs are one focus of Teaching Poster 5, introduced in Unit 13). Have students use the homographs in oral and written sentences.

Have students write (IN OTHER WORDS): "The present day is the critical day, because each day presents itself with the potential for being significant. Every day is life's present to you." Ralph Waldo Emerson

74

Build Skillful Writers

Use these interrelated language learnings for all or selected students.

Teaching Notes, page 328

Dictionaries show the correct spelling, meaning, and pronunciation of a word. Explore a dictionary pronunciation key, highlighting these word groups—

- Homographs (see Activity 2B, this unit) are words that have more than one pronunciation and meaning (e.g., present).
- Some words have more than one correct pronunciation (e.g., tomato, roof, aunt).
- Some mispronounced words result in their misspelling (e.g., government, library, February, sophomore, chocolate, surprise, pumpkin, probably, literature, asked, hundred, *candidate). Have students check their pronunciation in a dictionary. [*See Word Mysteries and Histories, page 79.]

Make three accordion class books (see page 394) to highlight each word group. Have students include a page for each word that shows its pronunciation, its meaning, and a sentence that uses the word.

Build Assessment Readiness

Use these at-school and at-home exercises to prepare all students for the Skill Test.

Teaching Notes, page 329

at-school Review *er*, the most common spelling pattern for the suffix meaning "one who" or "something that" (Build Skillful Writers, page 66). Then remind students that *er* can mean "more" (e.g., bright/brighter). Post Teaching Poster 2 to guide students through the suffix addition process.

Skill to be tested:
er suffix

Dictate these words for students to add the *er* suffix: *heavy, race, ship, rich, present, white, teach, listen, travel, plan, mow.* Later, write the words on the chalkboard, or have a student do so, for self-checking. Then have students sort the words by the meaning of the suffix: *one who/something that* or *more.* Next, students find and write more words for each category.

at-home Send home a copy of Take-Home Task 9 Blackline Master, page 76, with each student to encourage parent-child partnerships.

Skill to be tested:
er suffix

Build Proofreading Skills

Track students' ability to meet a minimum competency for spelling and proofreading within selected samples of their everyday writing.

Teaching Notes, page 330

- Send home papers for proofreading and a copy of the Ideas for Proofreading Blackline Master, page 373.

Name _____

Dear Parents,

Your child's word experiences, vocabulary, and spelling skills expand as your child masters how to add suffixes to words. This activity focuses on the addition of the er suffix, meaning one who (build/builder) or more (bright/brighter). The centerpiece for this practice is another analogy activity, a powerful exercise to help your child learn to think about words and their properties.

Have your child read and explain the directions to you. Then work together to complete the exercise. Take the time to discuss each analogy—ask your child why the answer is appropriate to ensure understanding. In fact, you and your child may wish to write more analogy exercises once you complete this Take-Home Task. The ability to write word analogies demonstrates a thorough understanding of them.

Complete the analogies using a word with the er suffix.

cut : scissors :: farm : f ___ ___ ___ ___ ___

circle : square :: blacker : w ___ ___ ___ ___ ___

walked : strolled :: shinier : b ___ ___ ___ ___ ___ ___

starting : stopping :: lower : h ___ ___ ___ ___ ___

middle : center :: thinner : s ___ ___ ___ ___ ___ ___ ___

question : answer :: sooner : l ___ ___ ___ ___

correct : right :: instructor : t ___ ___ ___ ___ ___ ___

furnace : warmer :: sugar : s ___ ___ ___ ___ ___ ___

simple : easy :: neater : t ___ ___ ___ ___ ___

schooner : canoe :: runner : j ___ ___ ___ ___ ___

north : south :: older : y ___ ___ ___ ___ ___

hike : hiker :: employ : e ___ ___ ___ ___ ___ ___ ___

sweeping : sweeper :: boxing : b ___ ___ ___ ___

build : construct :: chef : b ___ ___ ___ ___

Next, have your child write each of the analogy answer words on the back of this paper sorted by meaning: one who or more. Thanks parents—every child a speller!

Assess Words and Skills

- Spelling Words (words missed on tests) are recorded in the Spelling Notebook.
- Use Proof It, Practice Page 27, for proofreading/editing practice.

Teaching Notes, page 336

Assess Spelling Progress

Give this Cloze Story Word Test of Core Words within the frequencies 1–545 to all students. Words students miss are their Spelling Words.

 THE CLOZE STORY WORD TEST

Students do not prestudy the words. Provide students with a copy of REVIEW 9 BLACKLINE MASTER, page 80. Tell students that this is a story about dams. Dams are built in a unique way for good reason.

Read the entire story aloud, including the test words. Then read it again slowly as students write the missing words.

Devising a Dam

Dams have helped (1) <u>people</u> use water as a resource (2) <u>since</u> ancient times. Dams harness water for such things as irrigation, flood control, water storage, conservation, and power. The water power (3) <u>they're</u> able to produce is (4) <u>important</u>. Water is (5) <u>sent</u> through gigantic turbines to generate electrical (6) <u>energy</u>. Grand Coulee Dam on the Columbia (7) <u>River</u> is one of the greatest power producers in the (8) <u>world</u>. (9) <u>It's</u> made of concrete and, like other (10) <u>strong</u> dams, the convex side is by the water source. The dam curves, or bows, in a half (11) <u>circle</u> (12) <u>toward</u> the water. Engineers always (13) <u>plan</u> the construction of a dam in this way for a (14) <u>simple</u> reason. Why does the convex side of the dam need to be next to the water source (15) <u>rather</u> than (16) <u>its</u> concave side? Why don't they (17) <u>build</u> dams (18) <u>straight</u> (19) <u>across</u> the water supply? Please (20) <u>present</u> a (21) <u>bright</u> explanation for why dams are (22) <u>built</u> this way. Explain your answer by drawing a (23) <u>picture</u> to make your idea (24) <u>clear</u>.

Words tested:
its (76), people (79), world (191), important (195), picture (232), since (238), across (247), it's (253), toward (275), built (360), strong (381), river (394), simple (455), build (487), clear (510), energy (511), circle (519), straight (524), bright (541), sent (542), present (543), plan (544), rather (545), *they're (1010)

*The testing of they're (1010) is included to help students differentiate among the there/ their/they're homophones.

 AFTER THE CLOZE STORY WORD TEST

1. Have students locate Grand Coulee Dam on a map. Discuss convex/concave. Have students write and draw their explanation. Conclude that concrete dams are built with the convex side toward the water to make them stronger. Concrete may crack. If this happened, the concrete could break if the dam's construction had its concave side against the water source, and the concrete would be forced outward. With convex construction, the water source would force the concrete inward through compression, averting a break.

reasoning, writing, art

2. Have students record the words they missed on the test in their Spelling Notebook (see page 338) for at-school study, and on a copy of the WORDS TO LEARN BLACKLINE MASTER, page 375, for at-home study.

recording words for personal study list

Sourcebook 5, Unit 9

139

Teaching Notes, page 339

Assess Skill Application

Give this assessment of spelling and related skills to all students.
The Review 9 Blackline Master is on page 81.

🍎 **THE SKILL TEST**

Skill tested:
er suffix

Add the **er** suffix. Then write the meaning of the suffix.

plan	planner	one who	catch	catcher	one who
listen	listener	one who	blue	bluer	more
bright	brighter	more	clear	clearer	more
buy	buyer	one who	run	runner	one who
write	writer	one who	happy	happier	more
fly	flier	one who	farm	farmer	one who
straight	straighter	more	friendly	friendlier	more
box	boxer	one who	teach	teacher	one who

Note the ability of each student to write words with the *er* suffix and to identify the meaning of the suffix.

Teaching Notes, page 341

Assess Proofreading Application

Give this assessment of spelling and related skills to all students.
The Review 9 Blackline Master is on page 81.

🍎 **THE PROOFREADING TEST**

If any underlined word or words in each line are incorrect,
write the correction(s) in the space.

We know about shapes, such as <u>circles and squares</u>, and
we know about <u>the different</u> angles and curves of the lines
that make these shapes. Have you ever <u>thougt about</u> a   thought
melody <u>having a shape</u>? Melodies have shapes made of
lines going up and down that <u>you can pickture</u>. The shape   picture
of "Row, Row, Row Your Boat" begins with a <u>straght line</u>.   straight
<u>then it goes</u> up and comes back down. In longer songs,   Then
if you <u>listen carfully</u>, you may hear a melody repeat   carefully
itself. Sometimes when it repeats, the <u>melody is a littel</u>   little
higher or lower. The Star-Spangled Banner <u>has a very</u>
dramatic shape that suits <u>its' grand message</u>. The lines   its, message
of its melody go up high, bursting into the sky, <u>and than</u>   then
swoop down <u>agin like a soaring</u> eagle.   again

Think of a song you know, write the song's words, and then under the words draw
the lines formed by its melody.

Note the ability of each student to proofread for spelling and/or capitalization errors.

78

Extend Spelling Assessment

Give this in-context assessment of Core Words within the frequencies 1–545 to students who need more practice or challenge.

Teaching Notes, page 342

 THE SENTENCE DICTATION TEST

Students do not prestudy the words. Provide students with writing paper and pencil. Have students write the sentences as they are dictated.

> SENTENCE DICTATION
>
> 1. Tomorrow I'll present my written book report to my English teacher.
> 2. There's a chance I'll write it on bright blue paper rather than plain white.
> 3. Mrs. Brown plans to carefully check my work and listen as I explain it to her.
> 4. If it's in good form, then it will be sent to the library for other children to read.

Words tested:
the (1), and (3), a (4), to (5), in (6), it (10), for (12), on (14), as (16), be (21), I (24), there('s) (37), if (44), will (46), then (53), other (60), her (64), than (73), my (80), good (106), write (108), work (124), read (165), form (197), children (200), white (239), paper (241), it's (253), book (307), I'll (325), English (350), blue (407), carefully (427), check (493), listen (507), explain (513), teacher (539), bright (541), sent (542), present (543), plan(s) (544), rather (545)

Extra words: Brown, chance, library, Mrs., plain, report, tomorrow, written

 AFTER THE SENTENCE DICTATION TEST

1. Have students write a brief book report on a recent fictional reading. Have them suggest another ending to the story in their report.

writing a book report

2. Have students record the words they missed on the test in their Spelling Notebook (see page 345) for at-school study, and on a copy of the Words to Learn Blackline Master, page 375, for at-home study.

recording words for personal study list

Dictate this tongue-twister for students to write and say: There's no need to light a night-light on a slightly light night like tonight's night.

- Challenge students to write more sentences for dictation to twist their classmates' tongues.

WORD MYSTERIES AND HISTORIES

Long ago, Romans running for a public office wanted to make a good impression on the voters. To do so, they wore spotless, white robes when they gave speeches. The Latin word *candidatus* means "one who dresses in white," thus they became known as candidates. *Candidate* is often mispronounced and, as a result, often misspelled. (See Build Skillful Writers, page 75).

Word Test

Devising a Dam

Dams have helped (1) _____ use water as a resource (2) _____

ancient times. Dams harness water for such things as irrigation, flood control,

water storage, conservation, and power. The water power (3) _____

able to produce is (4) _____. Water is (5) _____ through

gigantic turbines to generate electrical (6) _____. Grand Coulee Dam

on the Columbia (7) _____ is one of the greatest power producers in

the (8) _____. (9) _____ made of concrete and, like other

(10) _____ dams, the convex side is by the water source. The dam

curves, or bows, in a half (11) _____ (12) _____ the water.

Engineers always (13) _____ the construction of a dam in this way for

a (14) _____ reason. Why does the convex side of the dam need to be

next to the water source (15) _____ than (16) _____

concave side? Why don't they (17) _____ dams (18) _____

(19) _____ the water supply? Please (20) _____ a

(21) _____ explanation for why dams are (22) _____ this

way. Explain your answer by drawing a (23) _____ to make your idea

(24) _____.

Skill Test

Add the **er** suffix. Then write the meaning of the suffix.

plan	_____	_____	catch	_____	_____
listen	_____	_____	blue	_____	_____
bright	_____	_____	clear	_____	_____
buy	_____	_____	run	_____	_____
write	_____	_____	happy	_____	_____
fly	_____	_____	farm	_____	_____
straight	_____	_____	friendly	_____	_____
box	_____	_____	teach	_____	_____

Proofreading Test

If any underlined word or words in each line are incorrect, write the correction(s) in the space.

We know about shapes, such as <u>circles and squares</u>, and _____

we know about <u>the different</u> angles and curves of the lines _____

that make these shapes. Have you ever <u>thougt about</u> a _____

melody <u>having a shape</u>? Melodies have shapes made of _____

lines going up and down that <u>you can pickture</u>. The shape _____

of "Row, Row, Row Your Boat" begins with a <u>straght line</u>. _____

<u>then it goes</u> up and comes back down. In longer songs, _____

if you <u>listen carfully</u>, you may hear a melody repeat _____

itself. Sometimes when it repeats, the <u>melody is a littel</u> _____

higher or lower. The Star-Spangled Banner <u>has a very</u> _____

dramatic shape that suits <u>its' grand mesage</u>. The lines _____

of its melody go up high, bursting into the sky, <u>and than</u> _____

swoop down <u>agin like a soaring</u> eagle. _____

Think of a song you know, write the song's words, and then under the words draw the lines formed by its melody.

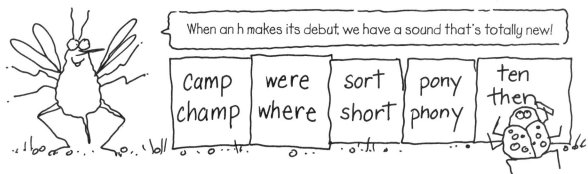

When an h makes its debut, we have a sound that's totally new!

| Camp champ | were where | sort short | pony phony | ten then |

Solve the puzzle with words that contain the digraphs ch, sh, th, wh, and ph.

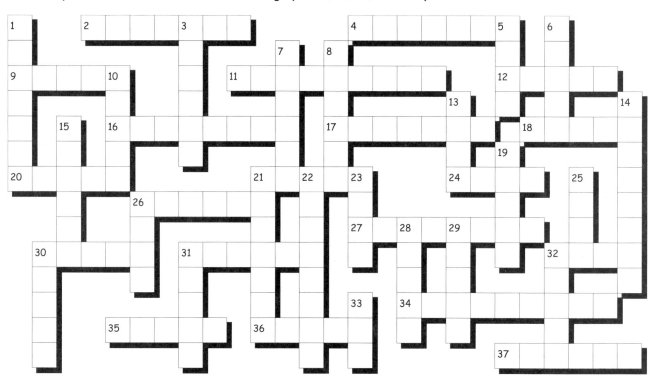

ACROSS

2. escape route for smoke in a fireplace
4. not your sister, but your ____
9. toss, pitch
11. fudge is often this flavor
12. kid
16. opposite of alone
17. feeling well; opposite of sick
18. attach this to your dog's collar before you go for a walk
20. not a comb, but a ____
21. the blade on this knife is dull, not ____
24. not now, but ____
26. to complete
27. common lunchtime food
30. footwear
31. look for, hunt for
32. slim, slender
34. use this to make a call
35. opposite of here
36. the bread was made today; it's ____
37. bikes have two

DOWN

1. soak in this to get clean
3. opposite of niece
5. wealthy
6. antonym for black
7. U.S. Independence Day is the ____ of July
8. mom, mommy
10. wear it on your wrist, it tells you the time
13. opposite of this
14. ten times one hundred equals one ____
15. a combination of breakfast and lunch
19. sandy area at the shore
21. wears a badge and arrests the outlaws
22. our 26 letters form this
23. opposite of pull
25. make a ____ upon a star
26. live in lakes, rivers, streams, oceans
28. opposite of south
29. largest mammal; lives in the ocean
30. yell, holler, scream
31. opposite of tall
32. not these, but ____
33. opposite of he

Now, sort your puzzle words in some way other than by the digraphs in the words. Label your categories. Next, add more words to each category.

I can **stretch** words by adding suffixes, and

I can **shrink** words by taking suffixes away.

Shrink these words. Remove the suffixes. Write the base words.

1. heavier _____

2. racer _____

3. shipper _____

4. richer _____

5. presenter _____

6. whiter _____

7. teacher _____

8. baker _____

9. traveler _____

10. planner _____

11. taller _____

12. simpler _____

13. hungrier _____

14. littler _____

15. sunnier _____

16. propeller _____

17. composer _____

18. writer _____

19. slipper _____

20. trespasser _____

21. listener _____

22. robber _____

23. crazier _____

24. employer _____

25. entertainer _____

26. funnier _____

27. gentler _____

28. flier _____

29. pitcher _____

30. safer _____

31. easier _____

32. stranger _____

33. earlier _____

34. later _____

35. speller _____

36. drummer _____

on another paper

Recall that the er suffix can mean—
        more: bright—brighter
    one who: win—winner
something that: heat—heater

Watch out! The suffix that means one who or something that is not always spelled <u>er</u>. It may be spelled <u>or</u> or <u>ar</u>—elevator, beggar. Make word cards for er, or, and ar-ending words, but leave out the vowel letter in the suffix. Then flash the cards to a partner who writes the words with the suffix. Next, it is your turn to write the words. Earn one point for each correct response!

VISIT__R

COMPUT__R

Circle three errors in each sentence. Then write the corrections.

1. A painter is a perrson who paints to make pitchers or someone who paints surfases to change or add color to things.

   _____   _____   _____

2. The Golden Gate Bridge in San Francisco is routinely painted to keep its finish colorfull, brite, and protected from the whether.

   _____   _____   _____

3. If you've not scene this mighty bridge, you might supose that its a golden color because of its name.

   _____   _____   _____

4. In fact, the bridge is realy a rusty shade of red that allmost seems to glow, especially on the foggyest days above the harbor.

   _____   _____   _____

5. Joseph strauss, the chief engineer during the construction of the bridge, said, "don't paint this grate bridge a boring shade of gray!"

   _____   _____   _____

6. So than, why is this California bridge named the Golden Gate Bridge when its color is certainlly not gold.

   _____   _____   _____

7. According to the San Francisco Historical society, the golden name means that this is a port that offers golden opportunitys for everyones prosperity.

   _____   _____   _____

You learned that the origin of the name of the Golden Gate Bridge has nothing to do with its color. Research the origin of the name of another bridge. Report your findings in writing. Give your report a beginning, a middle, and an end. Proofread! Then present your report orally to your classmates with a clear introduction, body, and conclusion to your presentation. You can do it!

Frequently Asked Questions

How long does it take to teach the Sourcebook methodology?

This is a frequent question, yet one that you are in the best position to answer. The Sourcebook is your source for developing your own spelling and word-skill curriculum. Each unit provides options to "customize" spelling and word-skill instruction and practice. What you choose to do in each unit depends upon your students and your goals. Following are factors that influence decisions:

What are the needs of my students?

If your students struggle with using the English language, for whatever reason, then target the Sourcebook's vocabulary development options—if students don't know "words," they struggle with reading, writing, spelling, and thinking. In the sidenotes of your units, note the references to vocabulary development. This includes lessons in idioms, etymologies, prefixes and suffixes, usage, grammar, homophones, homographs, synonyms, antonyms, onomatopoeia, Greek and Latin word parts, clipped words (bike), compound words, often-confused words (loose/lose, between/among), words with multiple meanings, similes and metaphors, abbreviations, contractions, irregular verb forms, onsets/rimes, and games that build comprehension and vocabulary. These would be good choices.

What is the focus of my school improvement plan?

For purposes of illustration, let's say the staff is working on increasing students' familiarity with classic literature. The Sourcebook can help you meet this goal. In Level 1 units, there's Relating to Literature, and although this is optional, use it. In all subsequent levels, see the many sidenote references to book tie-ins. In the back of each Sourcebook there is a list of all the literature included.

What are the strengths/weaknesses of other programs I'm teaching?

If your reading program is insufficient in providing a strong foundation in phonics, then select Sourcebook activities that are labeled phonics to strengthen this skill.

What does the Sourcebook offer to help me meet my state standards?

Many activities and exercises can be applied to state standards, which have been used as a guide for what to include, when, and how. Every state wants students to write and edit well, and every Sourcebook unit provides instruction and practice with these skills. For starters, you could select the optional Stretch It and Fix It activities that are included in each unit's Exercise Express.

Using these factors, as well as others that dictate curriculum and time frames, make your instructional decisions. Use the parts of each unit that help you teach your students what you think they need. If you do not complete all units, every word and skill is recycled next year in a fresh, new venue. Not to worry! Your goal is not to "cover" the book!

Having said this, there are sample lesson plans that follow on the next pages. But these lesson samples were made without ever meeting your students or knowing your needs or theirs! You'll make the best choices! Read on ...

One Teacher's Lesson Plans for a Five-Day Unit
Level 3, Unit 17 (without student Practice Book follow-up option)
(pages 122–131, Seminar Handbook)

Day 1 **Word Preview** (teacher-directed time: 5 minutes)
- For all students: Give/correct visual skill-building activity

Exercise Express (teacher-directed time: 5 minutes)
- For all students: Fix It—on chalkboard in AM; discuss and "fix" in PM
- For challenge: Find It—on chalkboard in AM, discuss in PM
- For homework: Stretch It—on blackline master, due next day

Day 2 **Exercise Express** (teacher-directed time: 3 minutes)
- For all students: Discuss homework Stretch It sentences; Sort It—on chalkboard

Seeds for Sowing Skills (teacher-directed time: 12 minutes)
- For all students: Activity 1B—Demonstrate *its/it's* "test," dictate sentences, "test" sentences, students correct; make *its/it's* word cards in AM, play word card game before lunch (word cards saved to replay)
- For challenge: Second part of Activity 1B, students write six *its/it's* sentences, share with partner
- For homework: Variant of Activity 2B—discuss silent *k* in *knew*; pupils find and write silent *k* words, due next day

Day 3 **Seeds for Sowing Skills** (teacher-directed time: 6 minutes)
- For all students: Discuss silent *k* homework words; variant of Activity 2D—review silent *t*, *w*, *gh*, *mb*, students find and write words with silent letters, share words with partner
- For challenge: Activity 2B—students find/write knock-knock jokes for class book (to be completed over next few days)
- For homework: Last part of Activity 2D—students make word chains that begin with silent-letter words

Day 4 **Seeds for Sowing Skills/Test Ready** (teacher-directed time: 10 minutes)
- For all students: Students share homework word chains with table group; do Test Ready at-school activity
- For challenge: Part of Activity 3A—students identify words that end in silent *e* to which *ly* suffix can be added; write rule
- For homework: Test Ready Take-Home Task blackline master

Day 5 **Cloze Story Word Test/Skill Test/Sentence Dictation Test** (teacher-directed time: 25 minutes)
- For all students: Give/correct Cloze Story Word Test—errors circled by teacher, students use copy of Core Words blackline master to fix errors, students do After the Cloze Story Word Test #2; Skill Test
- For challenge: Give Sentence Dictation to challenge students as others do After the Cloze Story Word Test #2; challenge students follow up with After the Sentence Dictation Test #1 and #2
- For homework: Words to Learn sheet goes home; assign After the Cloze Story Word Test #1—write words to "Happy Birthday" and another favorite song

...but remember,

you can grow your garden—

your way!

One Teacher's Lesson Plans for a Seven-Day Unit
Level 3, Unit 17 (without student Practice Book follow-up option)
(pages 122–131, Seminar Handbook)

Day 1   **Word Preview** (teacher-directed time: 5 minutes)
- For all students: Give/correct visual skill-building activity

Exercise Express (teacher-directed time: 5 minutes)
- For all students: Fix It—on chalkboard in AM; discuss and "fix" in PM
- For challenge: Find It—on chalkboard in AM, discuss in PM
- For homework: Stretch It—on blackline master, due next day

Day 2   **Exercise Express** (teacher-directed time: 3 minutes)
- For all students: Discuss homework Stretch It sentences; Sort It—on chalkboard;

Seeds for Sowing Skills (teacher-directed time: 12 minutes)
- For all students: Activity 1B—Demonstrate *its/it's* "test," dictate sentences, "test" sentences, students correct; make *its/it's* word cards in AM, play word card game before lunch (word cards saved to replay)
- For challenge: Second part of Activity 1B, students write six *its/it's* sentences, share with partner
- For homework: Variant of Activity 2B—discuss silent *k* in knew; pupils find and write silent *k* words, due next day

Day 3   **Seeds for Sowing Skills** (teacher-directed time: 6 minutes)
- For all students: Discuss silent *k* homework words; variant of Activity 2D—review silent *t, w, gh, mb*; students find and write words with silent letters, share with partner
- For challenge: Activity 2B—students find and write knock-knock jokes for class book (to be completed over next few days)
- For homework: Last part of Activity 2D—students make word chains that begin with silent-letter words

Day 4   **Seeds for Sowing Skills** (teacher-directed time: 10 minutes)
- For all students: Students share homework word chains with table group; introduce Activity 3A—students collect words to which the *un* prefix can be added, make a cumulative class list
- For challenge: Next part of Activity 3A—students write words that end in silent *e* to which *ly* suffix can be added; write rule, share
- For homework: Students do last part of Activity 3A

Day 5   **Seeds for Sowing Skills/Test Ready** (teacher-directed time: 8 minutes)
- For all students: Students read their homework sentences to their table group; do Test Ready at-school activity
- For challenge: Activity 3B—students work in pairs to write words to which *re* prefix can be added, alphabetize list
- For homework: Test Ready Take-Home Task blackline master

Day 6   **Cloze Story Word Test/Sentence Dictation Test** (teacher-directed time: 20 minutes)
- For all students: Give/correct Cloze Story Word Test—errors circled by teacher, students use copy of Core Words blackline master to fix errors, students do After the Cloze Story Word Test #2
- For challenge: Give Sentence Dictation to challenge students as others do After the Cloze Story Word Test #2; challenge students follow up with After the Sentence Dictation Test #1 and #2
- For homework: Words to Learn sheet goes home; assign After the Cloze Story Word Test #1—write words to "Happy Birthday" and another favorite song

Day 7   **Word Test and Sentence Dictation Follow-up/Skill Test** (teacher-directed time: 7 minutes)
- For all students: Student pairs read homework writing follow-ups; students who did the Sentence Dictation share follow-up writing with class; take Skill Test; do Cloze Story Skill-Building Extension #4; do Add It, and share with a partner
- For challenge: Cloze Story Skill-Building Extension #5; share with class
- For homework: Did You Know?—students identify different spelling patterns for /sh/

One Teacher's Lesson Plans for a Five-Day Unit
Level 5, Unit 9 (without student Practice Book follow-up option)
(pages 135–143, Seminar Handbook)

Day 1 **Word Preview** (teacher-directed time: 5 minutes)
- For all students: Give/correct visual skill-building activity.

  Exercise Express (teacher-directed time: 1 minute)
- For all students: Stretch It, Find It—on chalkboard in AM, students share with partner in PM.
- For challenge: Sort It—on chalkboard in AM, students share with partner in PM.

  In Other Words, page 73 (teacher-directed time: 1 minute.)
- For homework: Introduce quotation, assign, due next day.

Day 2 **In Other Words, page 73** (teacher-directed time: 3 minutes.)
- For all students: Discuss selected students' interpretations of the quotation.

  Seeds for Sowing Skills (teacher-directed time: 5 minutes)
- For all students: Activity 1A—in small groups, students list *ch* words (one minute). Make cumulative list on chalkboard, sorted by position of *ch* in word. Students follow up independently creating similar list for *sh*.
- For challenge: In Other Words, page 74.
- For homework: Activity 1A—students list *th, wh, ph* words, due next day.

Day 3 **Seeds for Sowing Skills** (teacher-directed time: 3 minutes)
- For all students: Activity 1A homework follow-up— have selected students write *th, wh, ph* words on chalkboard, sorted by the position of the digraph in the word. Discuss. Discover that no words end in *wh*.

  Build Skillful Writers (teacher-directed time: 4 minutes)
- For all students: Discuss the Day 2 challenge activity focusing on homographs.
- For challenge: Activity 2B—students find and write homographs, then write them in sentences.

  Test Ready (teacher-directed time: 5 minutes)
- For all students: Dictate words. Ask selected students to write answers on chalkboard for self-checking. Discuss meaning of each suffix: *one who, something that, more.*

- For homework: Test Ready Take-Home Task blackline master. Do the first two together.

Day 4 **Skill Test/Proofreading Test** (teacher-directed time: 11 minutes.)
- For all students: Give/self-check Skill Test; give/self-check Proof It.
- For challenge: Students continue Activity 2B, homographs.
- For homework: Assign Proof It writing follow-up, due next day.

Day 5 **Proofreading Test Follow-Up** (teacher-directed time: 3 minutes)
- For all students: Discuss homework, writing follow-up to Proof It.

  Cloze Story Word Test (teacher-directed time: 20 minutes)
- For all students: Give/correct Cloze Story Word Test— errors circled by teacher, students use copy of Core Words blackline master to fix errors, write spelling words on Words to Learn sheet and in Spelling Notebook.
- For challenge: Students hypothesize responses to story questions and write/illustrate their answers.

150

One Teacher's Lesson Plans for a Seven-Day Unit
Level 5, Unit 9 (without student Practice Book follow-up option)
(pages 135–143, Seminar Handbook)

Day 1 **Word Preview** (teacher-directed time: 5 minutes)
- For all students: Give/correct visual skill-building activity.
  Exercise Express (teacher-directed time: 1 minute)
- For all students: Stretch It, Find It—on chalkboard in AM, students share with partner in PM.
- For challenge: Sort It—on chalkboard in AM, students share with partner in PM.
  In Other Words, page 73 (teacher-directed time: 1 min.)
- For homework: Introduce quotation, assign, due next day.

Day 2 **In Other Words, page 73** (teacher-directed time: 3 minutes.)
- For all students: Discuss selected students' interpretations of the quotation.
  Seeds for Sowing Skills (teacher-directed time: 5 minutes)
- For all students: Activity 1A—in small groups, students list *ch* words (one minute). Make cumulative list on chalkboard, sorted by position of *ch* in word. Students follow up independently creating similar list for *sh*.
- For challenge: In Other Words, page 74.
- For homework: Activity 1A—students list *th, wh, ph* words, due next day.

Day 3 **Seeds for Sowing Skills** (teacher-directed time: 3 minutes)
- For all students: Activity 1A homework follow-up—have selected students write *th, wh, ph* words on chalkboard, sorted by the position of the digraph in the word. Discuss. Discover that no words end in *wh*.
  Build Skillful Writers (teacher-directed time: 4 minutes)
- For all students: Discuss the Day 2 challenge activity focusing on homographs.
- For challenge: Activity 2B—students find and write homographs, then write them in sentences, due next day.
  Test Ready (teacher-directed time: 5 minutes)
- For all students: Dictate words. Ask selected students to write answers on chalkboard for self-checking. Discuss meaning of each suffix: *one who, something that, more.*
- For homework: Test Ready Take-Home Task blackline master. Do the first two together.

Day 4 **Activity 2B/Build Skillful Writers** (teacher-directed time: 5 minutes.)
- For all students: Discuss challenge group's Day 3 homework—highlight pronunciations/meanings of homographs, identify consonant blends.
- For challenge homework: Ask a student to write words listed in third Build Skillful Writers activity on chalkboard—students check pronunciations of words in dictionary, write why mispronunciation may result in misspelling; due next day.

Day 5 **Build Skillful Writers** (teacher-directed time: 3 minutes)
- For all students: Selected students share Day 4's challenge activity—why mispronunciations can result in misspellings.
  Skill Test/Proofreading Test (teacher-directed time: 11 minutes)
- For all students: Give/self-check Skill Test; give/self-check Proof It.
- For challenge: Students continue Activity 2B, homographs.
- For homework: Assign Proof It writing follow-up, due next day.

Day 6 **Proofreading Test Follow-Up** (teacher-directed time: 3 minutes)
- For all students: Discuss homework, writing follow-up to Proof It.
  Cloze Story Word Test (teacher-directed time: 20 minutes)
- For all students: Give/correct Cloze Story Word Test—errors circled by teacher, students use copy of Core Words blackline master to fix errors, write spelling words on Words to Learn sheet and in Spelling Notebook.
- For challenge: Students hypothesize responses to story questions and write/illustrate their answers.

Day 7 **Word Test Follow-Up** (teacher directed time: 4 minutes)
- For all students: Discuss answers from Day 6 challenge activity (written and illustrated responses to Cloze Story Word Test questions).
  Sentence Dictation (teacher directed time: 5 minutes)
- For selected students: Give sentences, students self-check against correct sentences on chalkboard.
- For challenge: Students complete activity #1.

Plane English

Eye halve a spelling chequer
It came with my pea sea.
It plainly marques four my revue
Miss steaks eye kin knot sea.

Eye strike a key and type a word
And weight four it two say
Weather eye am wrong oar write
It shows me strait a weigh.

As soon as a mist ache is maid
It nose bee fore two long
And eye can put the error rite
Its rare lea ever wrong.

Eye have run this poem threw it
I am shore your pleased two no
Its letter perfect awl the weigh
My chequer tolled me sew.

-Sauce knot known-

Make a Step-Page Book

Each tier of a book is a <u>word collection</u>—
a prominent feature of the Sourcebook Series.
For example, a prefix step-page book houses
words with the prefix indicated on each tier.

Materials: three sheets of 8.5" x 11" paper,
             stapler, pencil.

Follow these directions to make a blank step-page book:
1. Place one sheet of paper flat on your desk.
2. Place the second sheet on top of the first sheet,
   1.5" below the top of the first sheet.
3. Place the third sheet on top of the second sheet,
   1.5" below the top of the second sheet.
4. Fold the three sheets of paper up from the bottom
   to 1.5" from the top of the third sheet of paper.
5. Now the papers should look like this—

6. Staple along the fold at the bottom.
7. Turn the papers so that the top is at the bottom.

Name _____

Word Preview

Print the words.

Print the words again.

_____   _____

_____   _____

_____   _____

_____   _____

_____   _____

Word Preview

Write

Rewrite

Print the words.

Print the words again.

_____

_____

_____

_____

_____

_____

_____

_____

_____

_____

Words to Learn

These are words your child has not yet learned. Use IDEAS FOR WORD STUDY to help your child learn these important words, not just for a test, but forever.

_____   _____

_____   _____

_____   _____

_____   _____

_____   _____

More Words for Super Spellers

These words go beyond the basics. You or your child may wish to add words here.

_____   _____

_____   _____

_____   _____

Name _____

Words to Learn

These are words your child has not yet learned. Use IDEAS FOR WORD STUDY to help your child learn these important words, not just for a test, but forever.

_____

_____

_____

_____

_____

_____

_____

_____

_____

_____

_____

More Words for Super Spellers

These words go beyond the basics. You or your child may wish to add words here.

_____

_____

_____

_____

_____

_____

_____

_____

_____

_____

_____

Name _____

Word Study Strategy

Write the words for study. Then practice the words for study two times. Follow these steps.

READ—Look at each letter of the word.
SPELL—Say the name of each letter of the word.
COVER—Cover the word so you cannot see it.
PRINT—Print the word neatly.
PROOFREAD—Check each letter of the word.

Words for Study	Practice	Practice
_____	_____	_____
_____	_____	_____
_____	_____	_____
_____	_____	_____
_____	_____	_____
_____	_____	_____
_____	_____	_____
_____	_____	_____

SOURCEBOOKS for Teaching Spelling and Word Skills

Description of the Research-Based Resource for
Teaching Spelling and Word Skills…Your Way!

The Sourcebook Series provides the infrastructure to craft a spelling and word skills program to meet your specific needs. It consists of one teacher resource book for each grade 1–8 that contains everything needed to craft your program. Nothing is consumable. Unit-by-unit menus of differentiated activities, tests, and blackline masters allow you to select what you need for teaching all the basic skills and concepts (see pages 52–59) necessary for spelling and word skill success. Optional student Practice Books for reinforcement and extension of selected Sourcebook activities are available for Levels 1–6 (see page 161), as well as a variety of program complements (see pages 162–166).

Sourcebooks are organized by grade level—and a kindergarten kit is underway!

- Level 1 for grade one teachers
- Level 2 for grade two teachers
- Level 3 for grade three teachers
- Level 4 for grade four teachers
- Level 5 for grade five teachers
- Level 6 for grade six teachers
- Level 7 for grade seven teachers
- Level 8 for grade eight teachers

Special Education teachers use the Sourcebooks at the reading level of the majority of their students.

Each Sourcebook—

- reviews all previous skills, concepts, and words,
- spans approximately one grade above and below the designated grade,
- contains *everything necessary* to teach the program,
- is a non-consumable teacher resource, and
- includes five, large Teaching Posters coordinated to activity ideas.

For examples of Sourcebook units and optional student Practice Book pages, see pages 122–146. Further, a complete unit for each Sourcebook and its optional Practice Book can be downloaded and printed from the website.

www.epsbooks.com/sittonspelling
888-WE-SPELL

REQUEST A FREE
OVERVIEW DVD OF
SITTON SPELLING AND WORD SKILLS.®

PRACTICE BOOKS for Learning Spelling and Word Skills

Description of the NEW optional student Practice Books
for collecting, analyzing, and learning about words.

Each Practice Book—

- correlates selected Sourcebook activities (2nd and 3rd Editions) with student tie-in exercises for Levels 1–6,
- includes a Proof It activity for every unit that parallels standardized format tests that assess spelling and all editing skills,
- features an "apple" extension activity on every page,
- all essential Sourcebook skills and concepts for a grade level are featured in the Practice Book,
- can be used with all or some students in regular education classrooms, in Special Education, for summer school programs, or as summer vacation at-home workbooks,
- lists all Core Words up to and including the grade level,
- provides a Priority Word list,
- includes a Spelling Notebook to record a running record of Spelling Words,
- features a page of rules for quick reference, and
- is priced cost-effectively and packaged in sets of five books; each package comes with a teacher reference that includes an Answer Key and chart of correlated Sourcebook activities for each unit.

For the Level 1 Practice Book—

- Just for first grade, there are 24 readiness pages, each with an extension idea, that precedes the implementation of Unit 1 in the Sourcebook.

Download and print a
Sourcebook unit and its
correlated Practice Book pages at
www.epsbooks.com/sittonspelling.

Now there's a
Practice Book with answers,
a teacher's answer key book!

SOURCEBOOK Teaching Posters and Personal Posters

Each Sourcebook for Spelling and Word Skills automatically includes a set of five Teaching Posters, each with an accompanying Personal Poster on a blackline master. Built-in ideas to use the posters are within the Sourcebook activities. Teaching Posters can be purchased separately.

Examples from Level 3

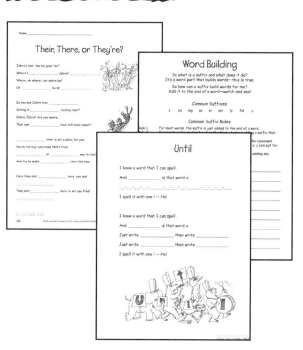

TUTOR ME Training®

- Video/CD-ROM training for either the 2nd or 3rd Edition Sourcebook Series to use independently or with a small group.
- Nine different programs:
  - Grade-specific, 1–8, for Classroom Teachers
  - Parent Introduction

162

MY SPELL CHECK® K-2

Your students' source for an alphabetical listing of 85 high-use writing words, with sections for animals, numbers, family, clothes, school, days, months, foods, and weather. Each coated card is 8.5" x 11", in color on both sides. Package includes 10 cards and a teacher resource of over 50 spelling and writing activities to extend the word bank.

SPELL CHECK® 3-8

Your students' source for an alphabetical listing of 150 high-use writing words, references for common abbreviations, days of the week, months, and 75 context sentences for often-confused words. Each coated card is 8.5" x 11", in color on both sides. Package includes 10 cards and a teacher resource of over 50 spelling and writing activities to extend the high-use word bank.

WORD-WISE SOURCEBOOKS

Your source for the best of Dr. Barbara Schmidt and Dr. Maurice Poe's laugh-aloud rhymes for learning spelling and language skills. Thirty-two blackline master poems and accompanying activities in each book escort students through difficult elements of spelling and language acquisition that complement the concepts in the Sourcebook Series for Teaching Spelling and Word Skills.

- Word-Wise Sourcebook One (Grades 1-2)
- Word-Wise Sourcebook Two (Grades 3-4)
- Word-Wise Sourcebook Three (Grades 5-6)

with

with #17 (Introduced in Level 1, Spelling...
Write, read, and spell with and every. Touch ea...
spelled aloud. Write: Everyone knows there cannot b...
raindrops and sunshine. Underline everyone, cannot, ra...
raindrops, sunshine, and identify the word parts of each co...
Have students create compound word equations on word card...
on a bulletin board: with + out = without, every + one = everyone.

Book Tie-In: Point out that grandmother, grandma, grandfather,
grandpa, and grandchildren are compound words. Share the
Caldecott winner, Song and Dance Man, by Karen Ackerman, in
which Grandpa has fun demonstrating his vaudeville routine to his
grandchildren. Then have students write a character sketch to describe Grandpa.
Students proofread their stories together, and compile them into a class book,
"About Grandpa."
www.sittonspelling.com

CORE WORD ACTIVITY CARDS

3.5" x 6" colored cards to correlate with grade-level Core Words, with activity ideas on the back of each card to make more words and extend the grade-level skills and concepts:

- Level 1: Cards for Core Words 1–35, plus 40 onset-rime pattern cards. Each card has an extension idea to complement the Level 1 Sourcebook skills.
- Level 2: Cards for Core Words 1–170. Each card has an extension idea to complement the Level 2 Sourcebook skills.
- Level 3: Cards for Core Words 1–335. Each card has an extension idea to complement the Level 3 Sourcebook skills.

WORD SKILLS in RHYTHM and RHYME for Levels 1–3

Six interactive rhymes and skill-building activities on each CD-ROM support each level's Sourcebook skills and concepts. Students work independently or in small groups for motivational spelling and language-related learning. Then, multiple print-out activities follow up the learning for more word work at home or at school.

- Level 1: Introduce your first graders to that dapper, dashing, and frolicsome Snappy Cat Jack to guide them through playful, interactive skill-building.
- Level 2: A frog named Zing, her family, and funny friends will have your second graders laughing and loving their concept-reinforcing lessons.
- Level 3: Laugh along with your third graders as bumbling, jovial General Spaghetti sits atop his portly horse, Meatball, and directs their language learning, and that of his brigade-of-one, Private Parmesan.

Learn to Spell the
Top 100
High-Use Writing Words

a	has	my	these
about	have	no	they
after	he	not	this
all	her	now	time
an	him	of	to
and	his	on	two
are	how	one	up
as	I	only	use
at	if	or	very
be	in	other	was
been	into	out	water
but	is	over	way
by	it	people	we
called	its	said	were
can	just	see	what
could	know	she	when
did	like	so	where
do	little	some	which
down	long	than	who
each	made	that	will
find	make	the	with
first	many	their	words
for	may	them	would
from	more	then	you
had	most	there	your

A complement to Sitton Spelling and Word Skills™ • ™ Educator Publishing Service • www.sittonspelling.com

100 WORD WALL CHART
(appropriate for all grades)
Your classroom source for the alphabetical listing of the top 100 high-use writing words. Each package contains five copies of this useful 18" x 24" chart.

It is within these 100 high-use words that most spelling errors are made. *There* and *their* hold the dubious distinction of being at the top of the "most misspelled or misused" list—even for college graduates!

SOME WORDS Vocabulary Mini-Course Series

There's a new kid on the block! Use the new mini-courses to help give your kids the single most research-supported advantage for academic and future success–VOCABULARY SKILLS! Limit one's vocabulary—limit their chance to succeed. For ELL and students of all ability levels—*vocabulary determines their achievement.*

Each Vocabulary Mini-Course is a 32-page consumable booklet, each page with an extension activity to do on another paper. Use independently or in a small group. No teacher prep time required.

- Non-grade-specific, for use with upper grades
- Each title comes in packages of 10
- Seven Mini-Courses
    SOME WORDS Have Suffixes
    SOME WORDS Have Prefixes
    SOME WORDS Have Latin Word Parts
    SOME WORDS Have Greek Word Parts
    SOME WORDS Are Often Confused
    SOME WORDS Are Homophones (Mini-Course I)
    SOME WORDS Are Homophones (Mini-Course II)

165